The New Mexico Mountain Bike Guide

BIG RING PRESS

The New Mexico Mountain Bike Guide

First Edition
© 1991
All Rights Reserved

-By-
Brant Hayenga and Chris Shaw

- Cover photograph -
Gooseberry Springs trail
Mt Taylor

- All photographs -
Brant Hayenga

PUBLISHED BY
BIG RING PRESS

Prepared by Christi Hield

All wanderers are made like this. A good part of our wandering is love, eroticism. The romanticism of wandering, at least half of it, is nothing else than a kind of eagerness for adventure. But the other half is another eagerness - an unconcious drive to transfigure and dissolve the erotic. We wanderers are very cunning - we develop those feeling which are impossible to fulfill. The love which actually should belong to a woman, we scatter among small towns, mountains, lakes, and valleys. We separate love from its object, the love alone is enough for us. In the same way that in wandering, we don't look for a goal, we only look for the happiness of wandering. Only the wandering.

Herman
Hess

CONTENTS

CONTENTS

INTRODUCTION

To use this book select a ride from the locater map or choose a ride from the appendix. The appendix categorizes the rides by difficulty. Each ride is ranked by two catagories; fitness level and riding skill. These ratings are based on normal route conditions. Snow, mud or rain can dramatically alter ride difficulty. Fitness level is a category that equates the strength and endurance necessary to comfortably complete the ride. Skill level is a category that mainly refers to the quality of the riding surface. Gravel roads are rated beginner, rocky single track trails are rated advanced. Most rides have some of each. Any of the rides in this book can be easily ridden if you know what your doing and plan ahead. Because many of these rides have both hard and easy sections we have tried to point this out so you can choose an appropriate ride. It is certainly appropriate to ride only a portion of the ride or get off your bike and walk any steep sections. An intermediate ride can be hard if there is a long climb. Refer to the ride graphs to make this determination. You can make a beginner ride hard if you really push, or you can make an advanced ride easy by walking the steep sections.

The fitness level and skill level ratings are very subjective and heavily influenced by weather conditions. We have tried to take these factors into account when we rated each ride. Ride distance is approximate, however the distances we list are very important for successful completion of many of these rides. We very strongly recommend that you use a good quality bicycle cyclometer. Do not rely solely upon maps, they can be outdated and inaccurate. We used cyclometers rounded off to a tenth of a mile to map these rides. It is almost essential that you use a cyclometer on any intermediate or advanced level ride. Riding time is also approximated and is influenced by many factors.

Riding time refers to the amount of time sitting on your bike. Lunch, breaks to fix a flat tire, and time out for pictures are not included in the riding time. Make sure you understand the entire ride description taking into account elevation, feet of climbing and weather conditions, before you choose a ride.

Many of the rides we describe are just one part of an elaborate network of old roads and trails. Remember a beginner ride can be turned into an all day adventure simply by making a wrong turn. We have choosen the rides we feel offer the best riding in a certain area. There are however many other opportunities for exploration. Make sure you have a map and compass with you before you do any backcountry exploration. Because many of these rides start or end on forest service roads you can change the mileage by parking in a different place.

We have indicated the amount of climbing to complete each ride. The elevation changes are shown on the elevation/distance graph in the ride descriptions. These elevation graphs approximate the cross section of the terrain for a given ride. All elevations are taken from topographic maps and are rounded off. You should be able to drive to the rides with the access information and complete the rides with the maps we list and the route descriptions given for each ride. In our access descriptions we assume a common starting point for each of the seven sections. They roughly correspond to the city or town closest to the area. All the information for indivdual rides assume you start or finish where we did. If you decide to deviate from these points the information given in this book will be affected. When researching these rides the authors found it impossible to mention all of the small side roads and forks. We only included the major intersections and forks that are necessary to complete the rides as described in this book.

All rides described in this book are located in a high altitude environment. Weather conditions may vary greatly in the time it takes to complete a ride. In the summer months at lower elevations hot temperatures and scarce water are typically encountered. In the high elevations afternoon thunderstorms can bring dramatic temperature drops and lightning hazards. During late fall, winter, and early spring, most of the high altitude rides are impassible due to snow. Always bring appropriate rain gear, warm clothes, food, water and survival gear. During hot weather more than two bottles of water will be necessary to avoid dehydration. Due to the extremely remote nature of these rides, bring all the necessary emergency bicycle repair tools to ensure your ability to return to your car. Equipment failure is not uncommon on more difficult rides. The most important piece of safety equipment is your helmet. Wear it at all times. We have described these rides as we found them in 1990. Somethings may have changed. It is your responibility to be aware of the changes, and it is your responsibility to be prepared for any given mountain bike ride.

REGIONAL RIDE AREAS MAP

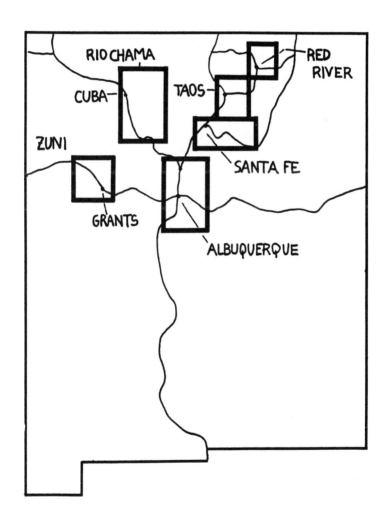

RIO CHAMA

RED RIVER

CUBA

TAOS

ZUNI

SANTA FE

GRANTS

ALBUQUERQUE

HOW TO USE
THIS BOOK

Honestly choose an appropriately difficult ride.

Buy and properly calibrate a bike cyclometer.

Purchase and study all appropriate maps listed in the
text for each ride.

The maps in the book represent the ride accurately but not all
roads and features along the route.

The roads and intersections necessary to complete
the rides are listed. However, for the sake of clarity
some small secondary roads have not been shown
on the ride maps.

Make sure your bike is in good working order.
Bring appropriate food, water, clothing and repair tools
for the length of the ride.

Always ride responsibly and respect other trail users rights
to have an enjoyable experience.

Ride hard and have fun!

MAP SYMBOLS

START OF RIDE -------------------- ★

FOREST ROAD --------------------- 10

HIGHWAY ------------------------- ⑤

INTERSTATE ---------------------- Ⓘ·25

DIRT TRAIL ----------------------

ROUTE DIRECTION --------------- ↑

STREAM ------------------------- ∿

RAILROAD ----------------------- ⊢╫╫╫

BUILDING ----------------------- ■

MTN SUMMIT --------------------- ☀

NORTH ARROW ------------------- ↑N

TURN AROUND POINT ----------

BRIDGE -------------------------

ALBUQUERQUE

ALBUQUERQUE

As the biggest metropolitan area in the state, Albuquerque offers the mountain bike enthusiast many opportunities not found elsewhere. Museums and a wide variety of restaurants are not the only reasons to mountain bike ride near Albuquerque. In fact there is so much good riding that some areas are becoming damaged from over use. We please ask that you ride with respect in these areas and try to minimize the impact by using different areas to ride.

The Alameda Bosque single-track takes the rider along the banks of the Rio Grande through an ancient riparian bosque. Riding through the cottonwoods you need to be quiet so you can hear the leaves whisper you a story. The 10K Loop near Placitas offers great views of the Sandias and is an easy beginner ride. The most popular area to ride near Albuquerque is around Cedro Peak. The popularity of this area is due to the large number of single track trails that are relatively free from rocks and the fact that it is only a half hour drive from town. This area can be muddy in the winter and spring and is best kept away from during these times. It also tends to be crowded on week-ends which is causing some environmental damage. Please try to be respectful when riding in this fragile environment. The Foothills Trail is on the eastern edge of Albuquerque, in the city's Open Space park and offers great single track riding next to town. The Faulty Trail on the edge of the Sandia wilderness is a good place to beat the heat in the summer. On the cool eastern side of the Sandia Mountains, this is a steep, challenging single track ride.

The best thing about mountain biking in the Albuquerque area is that half an hour drive away from a great ride you can eat dinner at a sushi restaurant and then go to a reggae concert at the El Rey theatre.

ALBUQUERQUE OVERVIEW MAP

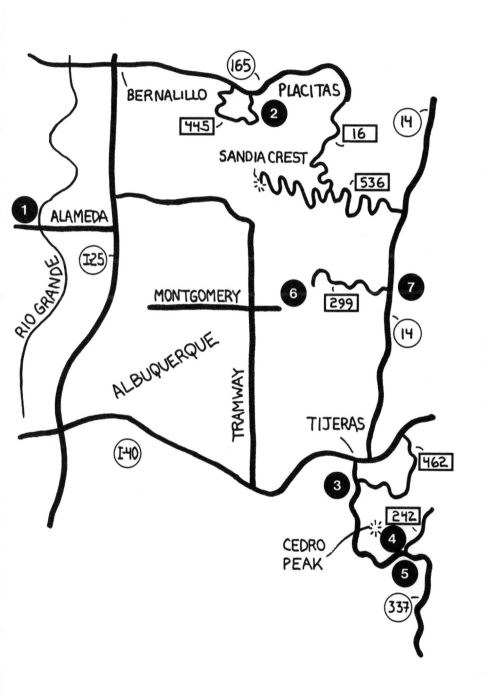

1   ALAMEDA BOSQUE
SINGLE TRACK

Total Distance: *12.0 miles*
Riding Time: *2 hours*
Elevation Gain: *100 feet in 12.0 miles*
Fitness Level: *Beginner*
Riding Skill: *Beginner*
Maps: *USGS 7.5' Bernalillo Alameda, Los Griegos*

LOCATION & ACCESS:
From Albuquerque drive north on I-25 and take the Alameda exit heading west. Drive down Alameda several miles and cross the Rio Grande. Just on the west side of the river is a wide dirt parking area on the right. Park here.

ROUTE DESCRIPTION:
From the parking area follow the ditch road as it goes through a gate and heads north. After only .1 miles you must cross the ditch on the small footbridge. After the bridge go over the levee on the far side and down into the bosque. The bosque is only a few hundred yards wide. On the east side is the river, and parallel to the river on the west is the ditch. In the bosque a series of trails head north. After about a mile you must ride up on the levee on the west to avoid a flood control barrier. Immediately after the barrier, you go back into the bosque. From here north you will cross several more barriers but these can be passed through without a need for diversion. At 6.0 miles from the car you reach a break in the bosque, turn around here and return via the same route.

ALAMEDA BOSQUE
SINGLE TRACK

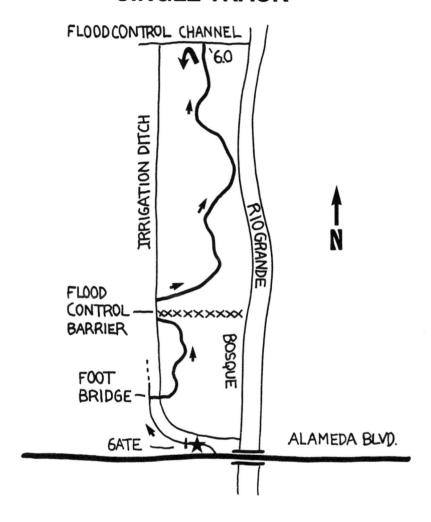

FLOOD CONTROL CHANNEL

'6.0

IRRIGATION DITCH

RIO GRANDE

N

FLOOD
CONTROL
BARRIER ── ×××××××

BOSQUE

FOOT
BRIDGE ─

GATE ─

ALAMEDA BLVD.

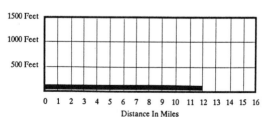

1500 Feet																
1000 Feet																
500 Feet																

0 1 2 3 4 5 6 7 8 9 10 11 12 13 14 15 16
Distance In Miles

2   10K LOOP

Total Distance:	*6.2 miles*
Riding Time:	*45 minutes*
Elevation Gain:	*500 feet in 1.5 miles*
Fitness Level:	*Beginner*
Riding Skill:	*Beginner*
Maps:	*USGS 7.5' Placitas, Bernalillo, Cibola Nat'l Forest Sandia District*

LOCATION & ACCESS:
Drive north from Albuquerque on I-25 18.0 miles and take the Placitas Highway 44 exit. Go right, east on Highway 165, 3.1 miles towards Placitas. Turn in on dirt Forest Road 445 on the right. Park .2 miles in on 445 at the strip mine trail head.

ROUTE DESCRIPTION:
Ride up road 445 heading south along the front of the Sandias. Road 445 climbs for the first 1.5 miles, at times moderate to steep, but after that there's almost all fast fun downhills. At 1.8 miles road 445A splits off on the left, stay right here. From here back to the junction with Highway 165, at 5.8 miles from the start. Don't ride up the hill on the pavement - there's a single track next to the road. Go up the single track for .2 miles and turn right on 445 back to the car.

10K LOOP

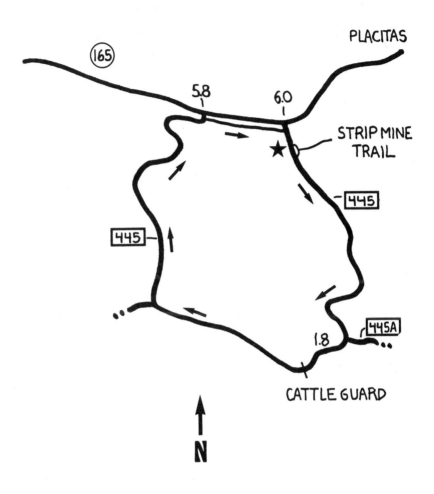

PLACITAS

165

5.8   6.0

STRIP MINE
TRAIL

★

445

445

1.8

445A

CATTLE GUARD

N

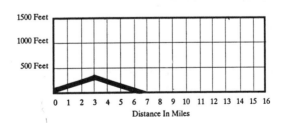

1500 Feet

1000 Feet

500 Feet

0 1 2 3 4 5 6 7 8 9 10 11 12 13 14 15 16
Distance In Miles

3 LONE PINE SINGLE TRACK

Total Distance:	*11.6 miles*
Riding Time:	*2 hours*
Elevation Gain:	*1000 feet in 5.0 miles*
Fitness Level:	*Intermediate*
Riding Skill:	*Intermediate*
Maps:	*USGS 7.5' Sedillo, Tijeras, Cibola Nat'l Forest*
	Sandia District
Notes:	*See Special Notes Section*

LOCATION & ACCESS:
Drive east on I-40 from Albuquerque to the Tijeras exit. Get off here and take the 337 South/Tijeras exit. Head south on 337 1.2 miles past the stop sign and park at the junction of 337 and dirt Forest Road 462 on the left.

ROUTE DESCRIPTION:
Ride up Forest Road 462 east away from the pavement. Road 462 begins to climb almost immediately. At .7 miles from the start turn right (this keeps you on 462). From here the road gets more rocky and continues to climb. At 3.1 miles from the start you arrive at a saddle, the junction with Road 13 is here. Keep straight on Road 462 (not right) over the saddle and after .1 mile you intersect Road 12. Go right on Road 12 and pass a fence line at 4.3 miles from the start. At 4.7 Road 12 turns up a steep climb. Opposite this on the left is Trail 11C. Turn left onto Trail 11C. This trail climbs at first then dips back towards Road 12, be sure to stay on the trail as it is one of the best single tracks around. At 6.7 miles from the start Trail 11C intersects Road 11, go left here. At 6.8 miles there is a split - stay right on #11. At 7.3 miles Road 11 bends to the left and climbs up a rocky hill. At 7.5 miles you intersect Road 462 (notice stone house ruin). Stay left heading up 462. 462 now heads back towards Road 12. At 8.3 miles from the start you arrive back at the 462/12 junction. Go right up 462, over the saddle straight ahead and back down 462, backtracking over the route you road up 462 on. At 10.9 miles from the start turn left (staying on 462) and rejoin the pavement and your car at 11.6 miles.

LONE PINE
SINGLE TRACK

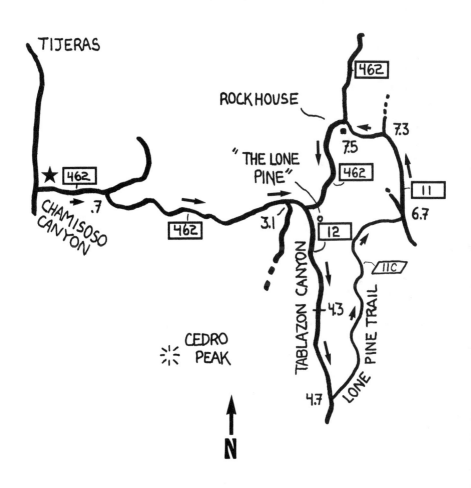

TIJERAS

ROCK HOUSE

462

7.3

7.5

"THE LONE
PINE"

462

11

6.7

★ 462

.7

CHAMISOSO
CANYON

462

3.1

12

11C

TABLAZON CANYON

4.3

LONE PINE TRAIL

CEDRO
PEAK

4.7

N

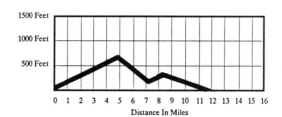

1500 Feet

1000 Feet

500 Feet

0 1 2 3 4 5 6 7 8 9 10 11 12 13 14 15 16

Distance In Miles

4 CEDRO PEAK SINGLE TRACK

Total Distance:	*6.5 miles*
Riding Time:	*1.5 hours*
Elevation Gain:	*200 feet in 3.0 miles*
Fitness Level:	*Intermediate*
Riding Skill:	*Intermediate*
Maps:	*USGS 7.5' Sedillo, Cibola Nat'l Forest Sandia Ranger District*
Notes:	*See Special Notes Section*

LOCATION & ACCESS:
Drive east on I-40 from Albuquerque. Exit on Highway 337, south to Tijeras. Drive past the stop sign up 337 through Tijeras. At 5.1 miles turn left on Forest Road 242. The sign says Juan Tomas and Forest Road 242. Drive up 242 .6 miles and turn left on the Cedro Campground, road 252. The road says private property but is actually public. Drive up this road 1.4 miles and park at the Cedro Campground on the left.

ROUTE DESCRIPTION:
This ride begins on Trail 252B which is across road 252 from the campground. There are two trails here - 252B is the lower trail on the right. This is a great single track with lots of turns and ups and downs. At 2.0 miles this trail intersects Road 252C. Go right here down .1 mile and intersect Road 12. Go left down Road 12 and at 2.3 miles from the start stay left on Road 12 (a right would send you on Trail 11C). Proceed along Road 12 and at 3.7 miles pass a side road on the left (stay right). At 3.8 miles you intersect Road 462, go left here. Climb 462 only .1 miles to the junction with Road 13 (at 3.9 miles from the start). Turn left on Road 13, which soon splits (4.0 miles from the start), stay right on Road 13. Now Road 13 becomes steep and rocky. At 4.8 miles from the start you intersect another road, stay right. At 5.0 miles from the start you intersect another road, stay right again. At 6.1 miles from the start you intersect Road 542. Turn left and descend down this broad road only .1 mile, then turn left on Road 252. Now descend on Road 252 back to the start at the campground, for a total of 6.5 miles.

CEDRO PEAK
SINGLE TRACK

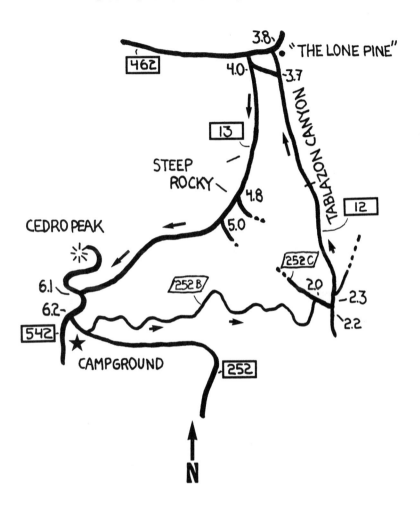

3.8
"THE LONE PINE"

462

4.0
-3.7

13

STEEP
ROCKY

TABLAZON CANYON

4.8

12

CEDRO PEAK

5.0

252 C

6.1

252 B

2.0

-2.3

6.2

2.2

542

CAMPGROUND

252

N

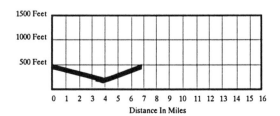

1500 Feet

1000 Feet

500 Feet

0 1 2 3 4 5 6 7 8 9 10 11 12 13 14 15 16
Distance In Miles

5 TABLAZON CANYON SINGLE TRACK

Total Distance: *11.7 miles*
Riding Time: *2-3 hours*
Elevation Gain: *800 feet in 5.0 miles*
Fitness Level: *Advanced/Intermediate*
Riding Skill: *Advanced*
Maps: *USGS 7.5' Sedillo, Cibola Nat'l Forest,*
                   Sandia Ranger District

LOCATION & ACCESS:

Drive east on I-40 from Albuquerque and exit on 337 south to Tijeras. Drive past the stop sign up 337 through Tijeras going south. At 5.1 miles turn left on Forest Road 242. Drive up 242 .6 miles and turn left on the Cedro Campground road, which is 252. This road has a "Private Property" sign but it is actually public.

ROUTE DESCRIPTION:

This road begins on Trail 252B which is across Road 252 from the Cedro Campground. There are two trails, take the lower trail (on the right as you face both trails). At 2.0 miles Trail 252B intersects Road 252C, go right here and descend .2 miles down a rocky section and intersect Road 12 at 2.2 miles from the start. Go left steeply down Road 12 and reach the bottom at 2.3 miles from the start. Now go right up Trail 11C. This excellent trail intersects Road 11 at 4.1 miles from the start. Go left on Road 11, and at 4.2 miles Road 11 splits, go right here. At 4.7 miles from the start Road 11 curves to the left and begins to climb. On the right is Trail 11D. Turn right off the road on to the trail. As you head down Trail 11D, at 5.2 miles from the start another trail branches off on the right, stay left. Trail 11D intersects Road 462 at 6.4 miles from the start. Go left up Road 462. As you climb up 462 you will pass several roads on the right - stay left on 462. There is now at short section of 462 that is closed to public access, you must find the "new trail" off of 462 on your left. This trail parallels 462 and rejoins it at 8.3 miles from the start. This is the junction of Road #11 (the left downhill) and 462. Go right on 462 past the stone house ruin. At 8.7 pass a fork on the right (stay left). At 9.1 miles 462 turns right - stay right. Climb .1 mile to a saddle and turn left on Road 13. Road 13 splits soon, stay right. At 10.1 pass 292C, stay right. At 10.3 stay right again. At 11.4 miles from the start you intersect Road 542. Turn left onto the road and immediately go left on Trail 240, which takes you back to the start.

TABLAZON CANYON
SINGLE TRACK

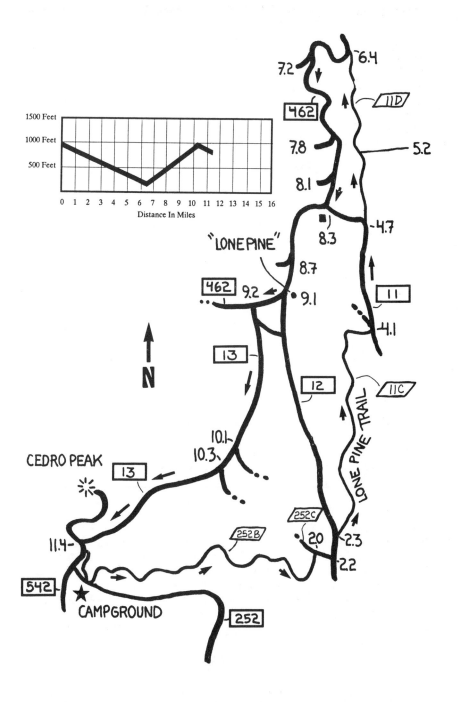

FOOTHILLS TRAIL

Total Distance:	*6.6 miles*
Riding Time:	*1.5-2 hours*
Elevation Gain:	*150 feet in 3.0 miles*
Fitness Level:	*Intermediate*
Riding Skill:	*Intermediate*
Maps:	*USGS 7.5' Sandia Crest, Cibola Nat'l Forest*
	Sandia Ranger District

LOCATION & ACCESS:
From the intersection of Montgomery and Tramway drive east on Montgomery .4 miles to the four way stop where Glenwood Hills intersects Montgomery. Turn left heading north .4 miles. Turn right onto a short unnamed road and drive towards the large cement water tank. This is the Embudito trailhead access area.

ROUTE DESCRIPTION:
From the Embudito parking area ride north through the passage in the fence. Head north on the Foothills Trail 365. Trail 365 continues north, crossing the paved Ellana Gallegos Picnic Area and eventually coming down into Sandia Heights at 4.5 miles from the trailhead. There are many side loops possible off of Trail 365. All of these loops are on the east (uphill) side of Trail 365. We have marked in miles the distance between each junction of all the possible loops. Now you can simply add together the different segments that you wish to combine into your days riding. Our favorite loop always includes Trail 305 because it takes the rider furthest up Bear Canyon.

FOOTHILLS TRAIL

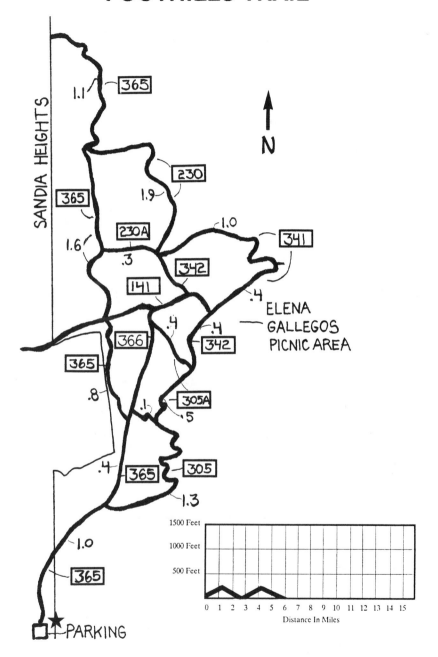

SANDIA HEIGHTS

365

1.1

N

230

365

1.9

230A

1.6

.3

341

1.0

141

342

366

.4

365

.4

.4

342

ELENA
GALLEGOS
PICNIC AREA

.8

.1

305A

.5

.4

365

305

1.3

1500 Feet

1000 Feet

500 Feet

0 1 2 3 4 5 6 7 8 9 10 11 12 13 14 15
Distance In Miles

1.0

365

PARKING

7 FAULTY TRAIL
SINGLE TRACK

Total Distance:	*13.0 miles*
Riding Time:	*3-4 hours*
Elevation Gain:	*1000 feet in 7.0 miles*
Fitness Level:	*Advanced*
Riding Skill:	*Advanced*
Maps:	*USGS 7.5' Sandia Crest, Sandia Park,*
	Cibola Nat'l Forest Sandia Ranger District

LOCATION & ACCESS:
Drive east on I-40 from Albuquerque to the Tijeras Exit. Go north at the split on Highway 14 towards Cedar Crest. After you cross back under I-40 go up Highway 14 3.5 miles and turn left on Forest Road 299 heading towards Cole Springs Picnic Grounds. Park here.

ROUTE DESCRIPTION:
Ride up road 299 heading west. After .2 miles the road splits, go right. At .5 miles from the pavement the road spilts again, go left towards Cole Springs. Soon the road begins to climb more steeply but is mostly middle ring. At 1.8 miles from the start, turn right on Canoncito Trail #150. Now begins the fun but highly technical and strenuous single track. Ride up Trail #150 until you reach the travertine pools and ledges, here you must push some. On top of the ledges is a level area by the stream. Here it is hard to follow Trail #150, just follow the stream up a few hundred yards more. At 2.7 miles from the start you intersect the Faulty Trail #195. Go right up this steep and rocky trail. For the next several miles this trail is highly technical and you will have to push in some sections. At 5.1 miles from the start just after a big drop, the Cienaga Trail #148 crosses the Faulty Trail. Stay on Faulty Trail. At 5.8 miles from the start, the Sulphur Canyon Trail crosses the Faulty Trail. From this point the trail is alot more rideable. At 7.3 miles from the start you "T" into the Oso Corredor Trail. Go right here down to the Bill Springs Trail and at 8.4 miles from the start you reach the pavement. Go down the pavement, through the Doc Long Picnic Area, and intersect the Crest Highway #536. Go right on 536 and intersect Highway 14 again. Take a right on 14 heading south and after 2.0 miles turn right and you're back at the car.

FAULTY TRAIL
SINGLE TRACK

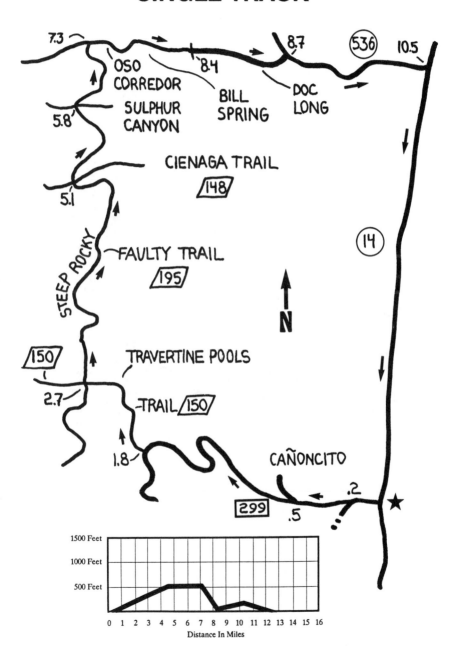

ZUNI REGION

ZUNI REGION

The rides in the Zuni region offer perhaps the widest variety of riding and scenery of any section in this guide. While most of the riding in this area is little more than an hour from Albuquerque, New Mexico's largest city, the area has remained mostly unused.

All of the rides for this section offer not only top quality riding and excellent views but also abundant variety. The Gooseberry Springs single track is certainly the most beautiful ride in the entire state, with views from the top of Mt. Taylor extending for 100 miles on clear days. El Calderon takes you back into the El Malpais National Monument, riding over the flanks of extinct volcanoes and just past the openings of some extensive underground lava tubes. The Zuni Mountain rides combine the two previous types: Mt. Sedgewick takes you through aspen meadows and rocky mountain tops, while Cerro Colorado and Quartz Hill remain lower in the sage, pinon, and juniper valleys crisscrossed with ancient lava flows. These later two rides occasionally take you through higher ponderosa pine and aspen groves as well.

Mountain biking is only one of the attractions to keep you coming back to the Zuni region. With Zunis, Navajos, Acomas, Lagunas, Hispanics and Anglos all living in the region, its cultural appeals are many. We strongly recommend side trips to Acoma Pueblo, Zuni Pueblo and Laguna Pueblo. The El Malpais National Monument has dozens of unique geologic and historical sites that should not be missed. Crossing the continental divide in the Zuni Mountains always gives us a thrill on our way over to El Morro National Monument. The Zuni region is the secret underdog of the west, sitting quietly unnoticed while everyone races north. We're sure once you've visited, you'll be back.

ZUNI REGION OVERVIEW MAP

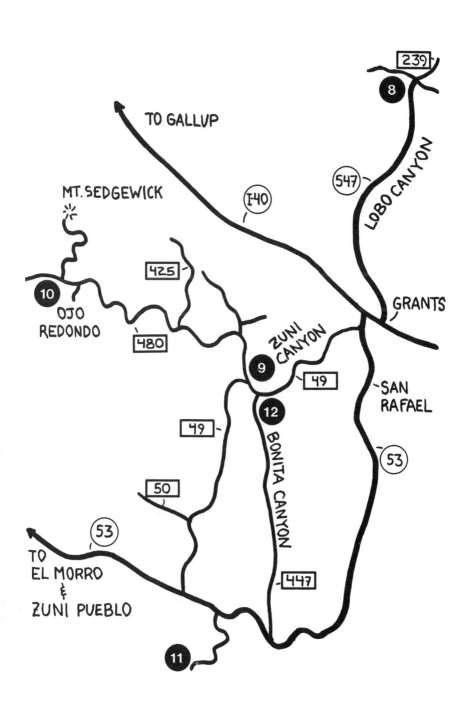

8 GOOSEBERRY SPRINGS SINGLE TRACK

Total Distance:	*18.7 miles*
Riding Time:	*4-5 hours*
Elevation Gain:	*3,100 feet in 10.0 miles*
Fitness Level:	*Advanced*
Riding Skill:	*Intermediate/Advanced single track descent*
Maps:	*USGS 7.5' Mt Taylor, Lobo Springs, San Mateo, Cerro Pelon, Cibola Nat'l Forest Mt Taylor*

LOCATION & ACCESS:
Drive west to Grants on I-40 and take the first Grants exit (Grants and Mt Taylor) Drive into town from this exit 2 miles on Santa Fe Ave. and turn right on 1st Street. Proceed one mile on 1st Street and turn right on 547. Go 1/2 mile to traffic light and go left (still 547). Now drive up 547, 13 miles to the end of the pavement and park.

ROUTE DESCRIPTION:
When the pavement ends on 547 it becomes Forest Road 239. Ride up 239 3.5 miles and look for Road 493 on the right. Turn right here heading towards La Mosca saddle on 453. At 5.8 miles from the start the road forks, go right staying on 453. La Mosca saddle is reached at 8.1 miles from the start. At the saddle there are 3 options; first is the La Mosca Peak turn on the left, then a little further are the other two. Take a right uphill (not the left downhill or the trail) which is Road 570. The road climbs until you reach a small saddle at 10.0 miles from the car. Here the rider must look very closely on the left to find Trail 77 up to the top of Mount Taylor. The trail climbs steeply for .3 miles and the top is reached at 10.3 miles from the start. The Gooseberry Trail 77 continues down the south side of Mount Taylor down a large open meadow. At the top (11,301 feet) the trail is hard to find but just below it is easy to follow. Ride down Trail 77 (watch for gate and fence half way down) and at 13.0 miles the trail crosses an old road. Keep on the trail which is sometimes hard to follow as it turns to the right as soon as it crosses the road. This last .7 miles of the trail is technical, with some short uphills. Intersect Road 193 at 13.6 miles from the start. Turn right here and descend down Road 193 the 5.1 miles to the car.

GOOSEBERRY SPRINGS
SINGLE TRACK

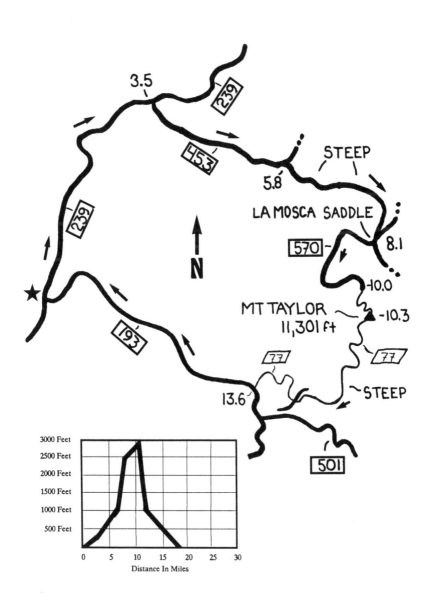

9 CERRO COLORADO

Total Distance: 11.6 miles
Riding Time: 2 hours
Elevation Gain: 650 feet in 7.0 miles
Fitness Level: Intermediate
Riding Skill: Beginner
Maps: USGS 7.5' Mt. Sedgewick, Paxton Springs, Cibola Nat'l Forest (Mt. Taylor)

LOCATION & ACCESS:
From Albuquerque take I-40 west and exit on Highway 53 heading towards Zuni. After crossing over I-40 you only drive 100 yards on Highway 53 then turn right on Zuni Canyon Road (next to the Zuni Canyon Trading Post). Drive up Zuni Canyon, which starts out as a paved road but becomes gravel road 49 after 4.5 miles. Drive on, at 11.0 from 53 the road splits, go right here staying on 49. Drive another .9 miles to the next fork and park.

ROUTE DESCRIPTION:
Begin this ride at the fork of 49/480 where you parked. Go right up road 480 and after 1.9 miles you reach a bend in the road. On this bend there is a road on the right. Take this turn on to Limekiln Canyon Road. Ride up this road .1 miles and take the left hand fork which keeps you going up Limekiln Canyon. At 4.0 miles from the start pass a road on the right, but stay straight. Keep riding up Limekiln until a left turn is reached at 4.6 miles from the start. Go left here and descend across a valley and intersect road 425 at 5.0 miles from the start. Turn left here and gradually climb up road 425 towards Cerro Colorado. At about 7.0 miles from the start road 425 begins to descend back towards road 480. You will pass an old water tank on the right just before you reach road 480 at 7.8 miles from the start. Turn left and descend the remaining 3.8 miles on road 480 back to the car.

CERRO
COLORADO

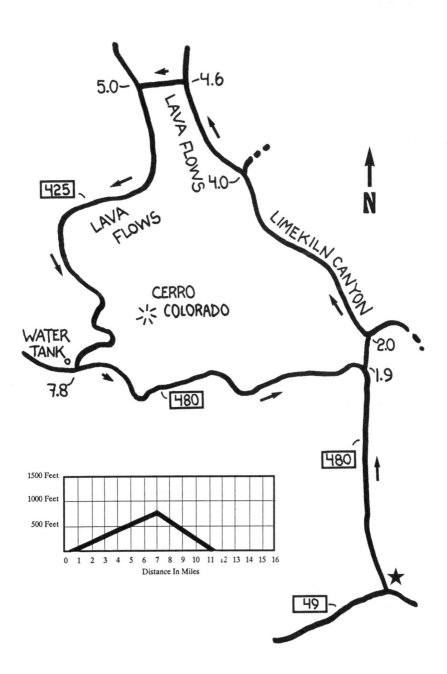

10 MT SEDGEWICK

Total Distance:	*8.5 miles*
Riding Time:	*1.5-2 hours*
Elevation Gain:	*700 feet in 2.8 miles*
Fitness Level:	*Beginner, except for the .8 mile optional side trip to the Mt Sedgewick summit*
Riding Skill:	*Beginner*
Maps:	*USGS 7.5' Post Office Flat, Mt Sedgewick, Cibola Nat'l Forest Mt Taylor*

LOCATION & ACCESS:
From I-40 west take the Highway 53 exit heading towards Zuni Pueblo. After crossing over I-40 you only drive 100 yards on Highway 53, then turn right on Zuni Canyon Road (next to the Zuni Canyon Trading Post). Drive up Zuni Canyon which starts as pavement but becomes gravel road 49 after 4.5 miles. Drive on at 11.0 from 53 the road splits, go right staying on 49. Drive another .9 miles to the next fork, go right again on road 480, heading towards Ojo Redondo Campground. Drive 8.0 miles up 480 and turn left. Park in the Ojo Redondo Campground.

ROUTE DESCRIPTION:
Start this ride from the campground and go left on 480. After .5 miles turn right on road 504; look for the old log cabin at this junction. At 2.0 miles from the start you intersect road 504A (here we recommend the short side trip up the steep rocky .8 miles to the actual summit of Mt Sedgewick). If you do the side trip to the summit of Mt. Sedgewick turn right when you return to 504. Ride down 504 for a beautiful fast descent. Intersect road 178 at 4.5 from the start (mileages exclude side round trip to top). Go left here up the broad, smooth road 178 and intersect 480 again at 6.0 miles from the start. Go left up along aspen meadows and return to the Ojo Redondo Campground at 8.5 miles.

MT SEDGEWICK

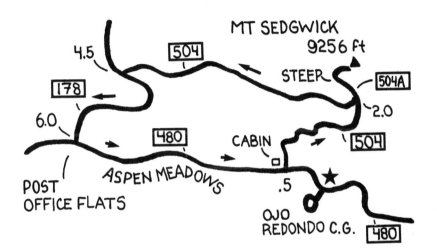

MT SEDGWICK 9256 ft

STEER

504A

2.0

504

4.5

504

178

6.0

480

CABIN

POST OFFICE FLATS

ASPEN MEADOWS

.5

★

OJO REDONDO C.G.

480

N

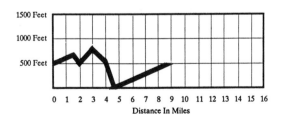

1500 Feet

1000 Feet

500 Feet

0 1 2 3 4 5 6 7 8 9 10 11 12 13 14 15 16

Distance In Miles

11 EL CALDERON LOOP

Total Distance:	*11.0 miles*
Riding Time:	*2 hours*
Elevation Gain:	*300 feet in 5.0 miles*
Fitness Level:	*Intermediate*
Riding Skill:	*Intermediate*
Maps:	*USGS 7.5' Ice Caves*
Notes:	*See Special Notes Section*

LOCATION & ACCESS:
Drive south from Grants on Highway 53 18.3 miles and turn left into the El Calderon area of the El Malpais National Monument. Drive in .3 miles on the dirt road and park at the gravel parking area.

ROUTE DESCRIPTION:
At the gravel parking area a road branches off on the right. Ride up the road heading towards the Cerritos De Jaspe on an intermittently rocky road. At .8 miles from the start the road splits, go left following the dead end sign. The road climbs up the side of the El Calderon Volcano and at 1.5 miles there are great views off to the east across the Malpais to the La Ventana Cliffs. The road drops off the back side of the volcano and you must pass through a gate and descend into an open valley. As you near the valley floor you see a road you will intersect at 2.4 miles from the start. The two roads join. Keep going and 100 feet later a road splits on the left, stay right here and soon the road is climbing up the Cerritos De Jaspe. At 3.4 miles from the start you reach the top and begin the descent down the back side. As you descend stay on the left side of the fence line. At 4.4 miles from the start you reach the bottom and a junction. Go right here, climbing up the steep and rocky hill. Now there is a series of ups and downs with many small side roads branching off the road you are on. The road goes along with the lava on the left and the Cerritos on the right. At 7.4 miles, the road splits off on the left, stay right. At 7.6 miles you pass another fence and enter back into the El Calderon area. At the split at 8.4 miles go right.. At 9.1 miles a side road bends off on the right, stay left here and go up some small hills. At 10.1 you are back to the first split. Keep left here and descend the .8 miles back to the parking area, for a total distance of 11.0 miles.

EL CALDERON
LOOP

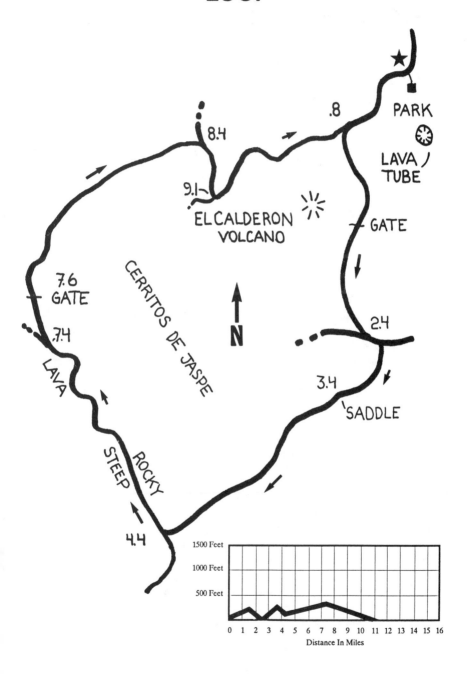

12 QUARTZ HILL

Total Distance:	*7.3 miles*
Riding Time:	*1.5 hours*
Elevation Gain:	*400 feet in 4.0 miles*
Fitness Level:	*Intermediate/Beginner*
Riding Skill:	*Beginner*
Maps:	*USGS 7.5' Paxton Springs, Cibola Nat'l Forest*
	Mt. Taylor District

LOCATION & ACCESS:
From Albuquerque take I-40 west and exit on Highway 53 heading towards Zuni. After crossing over I-40 you only drive 100 yards on Highway 53 then turn right on Zuni Canyon Road (next to the Zuni Canyon Trading Post). Drive up Zuni Canyon, which starts out as a paved road but becomes gravel road 49 after 4.5 miles. Drive on, at 11.0 miles from Highway 53 the road splits. This is the junction (49/447) between Zuni Canyon and Bonita Canyon. Park here.

ROUTE DESCRIPTION:
From this junction go left and head south down Bonita Canyon. Watch closely on the right, and turn on the two track road .2 miles from the start (be sure to pass the two track on the right at .1 miles along 447). Now ride up the two track and soon it enters a beautiful canyon where the ancient lava flows poured into Zuni Canyon. This road climbs along this canyon and at 3.4 miles you pass a side fork on the right (this fork dead ends into a mine area). Now begins some steep, rocky sections. At 3.6 miles from the start you reach a saddle. Go left here up the hill (going straight sends you down the wrong side of the saddle). Now the road still climbs but is only moderately steep. At 4.4 miles from the start pass a side road to a mine on the left. From here begins the fun descending, with a few short climbs thrown in. At 6.4 miles from the start you intersect the Bonita Canyon Road again. Go left here back up Bonita Canyon and reach the car at 7.3 miles.

QUARTZ HILL

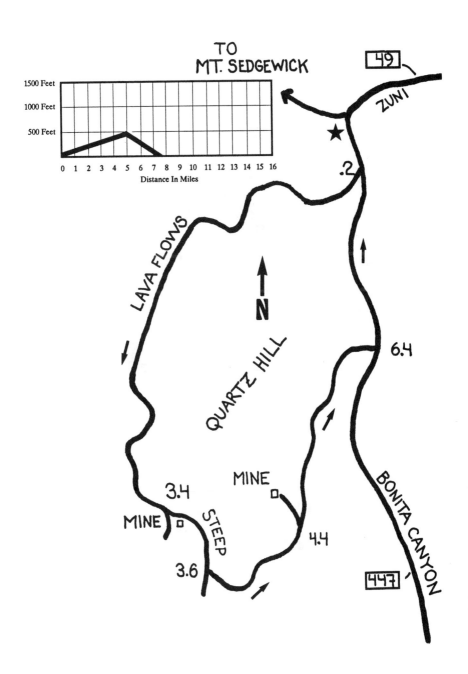

TO
MT. SEDGEWICK

49

ZUNI

1500 Feet
1000 Feet
500 Feet

0 1 2 3 4 5 6 7 8 9 10 11 12 13 14 15 16
Distance In Miles

.2

LAVA FLOWS

N

QUARTZ HILL

6.4

MINE

3.4

MINE

STEEP

4.4

3.6

BONITA CANYON

447

SANTA FE

SANTA FE

What can we say about Santa Fe that hasn't already
been said too many times in tourist brochures in New York
City? In spite of the recent hype, Santa Fe really is an elegant
city filled with a unique mix of eclectic and eccentric people.
Santa Fe is the gateway to the highcountry and the southern
guardian of the Sangre De Cristo Mountains.

We had difficulty finding a mixed group of beginner,
intermediate and advanced rides from Santa Fe (there are lots
of advanced rides) but in the end the mix is great. Glorieta
Baldy is a fun but difficult ride to the top of the mountain
(complete with a forest lookout) and true to our favorite
format you get miles of downhill single-track. Glorieta Mesa
on the other hand is a really nice beginner area that is close to
town. The Barillas Peak Lookout ride takes you through
several small rural villages and to the top of Barillas Peak
for big views. Still evident around the peak are the scars from
the cat and dog fires in the 1970's. Aspen Vista and Elk
Mountain take you higher still, through the archetypal forests
of your secret 9 to 5 mountain bike fantasies (hard riding in
cool mountain meadows with beautiful young naked
bodies....oops, endorphin flashbacks). The Lamy Railroad
single track starts right in town and while not physically difficult, it gives the beginner rider good practice for the more
advanced and technical rides. Guaje Canyon is somewhat of a
departure, taking you to Los Alamos and the Jemez Mountains
but is accessed easily from Santa Fe.

After hours of great riding returning to town for a
huge New Mexican dinner is first on our agenda. And after
dinner, soaking in the Japaneese baths at Ten Thousand
Waves with a jug of cheap red wine always sends us -
but that's another story.

SANTA FE OVERVIEW MAP

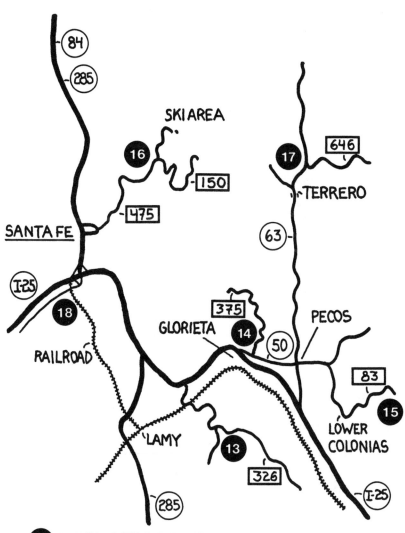

13 GLORIETA MESA

Total Distance:	*10.0 miles*
Riding Time:	*2 hours*
Elevation Gain:	*200 feet in 5.0 miles*
Fitness Level:	*Beginner*
Riding Skill:	*Beginner*
Maps:	*USGS 7.5' Glorieta, Santa Fe Nat'l Forest*
Notes:	*See Special Notes Section*

LOCATION & ACCESS:

Drive north on I-25 from the St. Francis exit in Santa Fe 7.4 miles and take the Lamy/Vaughn exit. Turn left here crossing back under I-25 and intersecting the frontage road. Turn right on the frontage road and drive 2.2 miles. Turn right on to the dirt county road 51, which passes back under I-25. This road is rough at first but gets smoother. After crossing the railroad tracks 1.5 miles in on the dirt turn right and go up the mesa. At 3.7 miles on the dirt (and on top of the mesa) the road splits. Go left onto Forest Road 326. Drive 1.0 miles on 326, when you pass a fence line there is a sign showing you are now in the national forest. Park here.

ROUTE DESCRIPTION:

Ride along 326 as it gently climbs and descends across the top of Glorieta Mesa. There are dozens of small side roads off of 326 that offer excellent riding, but are often confusing, so be careful, if you choose to try these side roads. At 4.2 miles from the start turn left on Forest Road 612. Road 612 has a short, steep rocky downhill near the intersection, but levels nicely. The edge of the mesa is reached at 5.0 miles from the start. Return to the car via the same route.

GLORIETA MESA

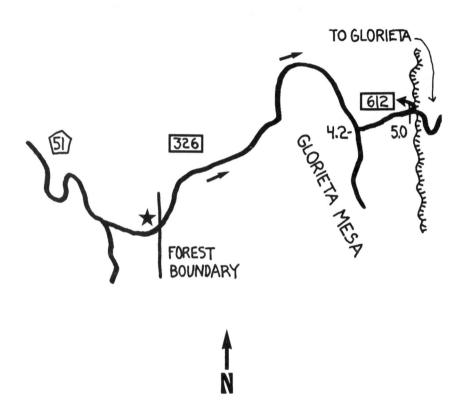

TO GLORIETA

51

326

612

GLORIETA MESA

4.2

5.0

★

FOREST
BOUNDARY

N

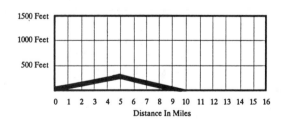

1500 Feet
1000 Feet
500 Feet

0 1 2 3 4 5 6 7 8 9 10 11 12 13 14 15 16
Distance In Miles

14   GLORIETA BALDY SINGLE TRACK

Total Distance:	*20.4 miles*
Riding Time:	*4 hours*
Elevation Gain:	*3000 feet in 11.9 miles*
Fitness Level:	*Advanced*
Riding Skill:	*Intermediate ascent, advanced single track descent.*
Maps:	*USGS 7.5' Pecos, Rosilla Peak, Glorieta, McClure Reservoir, Santa Fe Nat'l Forest*
Notes:	*See Special Notes Section*

LOCATION & ACCESS:
Drive north on I-25 from the St. Francis exit in Santa Fe 16.6 miles and exit on the Glorieta/Pecos exit. Turn left and cross back over I-25 to intersect Highway 50. Turn right on Highway 50 heading towards Pecos. Drive 2.0 miles and turn left on Forest Road 375 (this is not far beyond the Civil War Museum). Park at the 375/50 intersection.

ROUTE DESCRIPTION:
Ride up 375 from the car, climbing above the small town of La Cueva. At 7.0 miles the road forks, go left. At 8.0 miles the road forks again, go left. At 8.5 miles, near the stream and meadow the road forks yet another time, again go left. From here the climbing gets very steep and rocky all the way to the top of Glorieta Baldy. The top is reached at 11.9 miles from the start. Go past the picnic area all the way to the very top and the lookout. You will find Trail #272 on top near the lookout. The first 1/2 mile of the descent is mostly unrideable but keep on because the remainder is excellent. Pass the Broken Arrow Trail on the left at 15.6 miles from the start. Shortly after this is a section of the trail that is hard to navigate (in a bunch of sandstone rocks). At 16.6 miles from the start you intersect a dirt road, go right. This road descends into the Baptist Conference Center, and after a gate, the road becomes paved. Be sure to close the gate behind you. Ride out of the Baptist Center through the front gates. This puts you back onto Highway 50. Turn left and ride the 2 miles on pavement back to your car.

GLORIETA BALDY
SINGLE TRACK

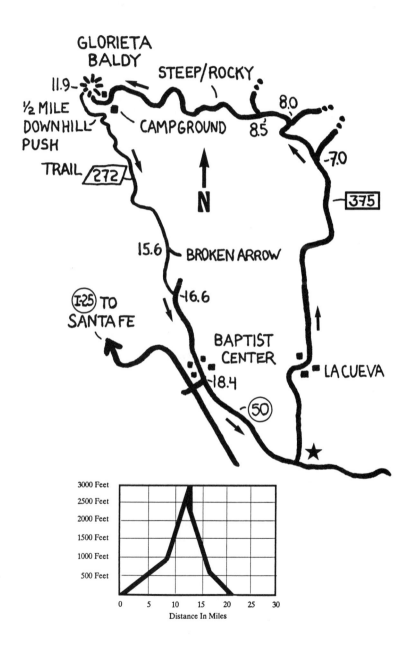

15 BARILLAS PEAK LOOKOUT

Total Distance:	*20.0 miles*
Riding Time:	*3-4 hours*
Elevation Gain:	*1300 feet in 9.0 miles*
Fitness Level:	*Intermediate/Advanced*
Riding Skill:	*Intermediate*
Maps:	*USGS 7.5' Lower Colonias, San Geronimo*
	Santa Fe Nat'l Forest

LOCATION & ACCESS:
Drive north on I-25 16.6 miles from the St. Francis exit in Santa Fe to the Glorieta/Pecos exit. After exiting cross over the overpass and go right on Highway 50. Drive 6.0 miles to the town of Pecos. As Highway 50 enters Pecos you come to a 4 way stop. As you proceed straight through the stop the road is now 223. Drive 3.2 miles on 223 and turn right on county gravel road B44A. This road goes up the ridge and down into the Colonias Valley. At 5.5 miles from the pavement the road splits, go right. Now the road is numbered Forest Road 83 and climbs up Ruidoso Ridge and at 9.5 miles from the pavement park at the 3 way junction on top.

ROUTE DESCRIPTION:
From the 3 way intersection proceed straight ahead on Forest Road 83 as it climbs gradually towards Barillas Peak. Pass the Apache Canyon Road 82 after 1.0 miles, keep straight. At 5.2 you pass the Aspen Wilding Area Road on the left, keep straight as road 83 crosses Sebadilla Creek. From here 83 climbs more steeply up a rocky road bed. At 6.6 miles from the start turn right and go down road 626. This road loops around Barillas Peak. At 9.0 miles (2.4 on 626) the road forks, take the left uphill fork, up the steep and rocky hill. At 9.5 miles you intersect road 83 again. If you go right you descend down 83 past where you turned off, and continue back to the car on the same route in. But first, take the side trip up to the top of Barillas Peak by going left, past the gate up to the top. Then descend 83 all the way back to the car.

BARILLAS PEAK
LOOKOUT

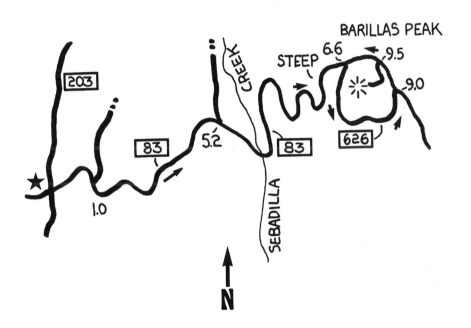

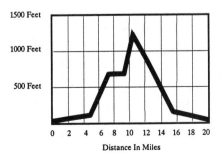

16 ASPEN VISTA

Total Distance:	*12.0 miles*
Riding Time:	*2-3 hours*
Elevation Gain:	*2000 feet in 6.0 miles*
Fitness Level:	*Advanced*
Riding Skill:	*Intermediate*
Maps:	*USGS 7.5' Aspen Basin, Santa Fe Nat'l Forest*

LOCATION & ACCESS:
From the Santa Fe plaza drive north on Washington Ave. approximately 1 mile. Just north of the Scottish Rite temple turn right onto Artist Road which is the Hyde Park Santa Fe Ski Basin road now numbered NM 475. Drive approximately 13.5 miles on NM 475 - just past the 13 mile marker and turn off to your right into the Aspen Vista parking lot.

ROUTE DESCRIPTION:
Start riding from the east side of the parking lot which has a gate across the road which is now numbered 150. The first 2.5 miles are through a large aspen forest which is beautiful in the fall. At .8, 1.6 and 2.3 miles you cross small tributaries of Big Tesuque Creek. Just past the last creek crossing, the road makes a big switchback and continues uphill into the mixed spruce and fir forest. At 3.8 miles the road crosses a large open meadow with good views of the Rio Grande Valley. At 5.0 miles after riding through a few more switchbacks the road again makes a big turn to the north and enter the forest. At 5.5 miles the road enters another large meadow. At this point you can look down on top of the ski lifts of the Santa Fe Ski Area. The top of Tesuque Peak with the microwave towers is reached at 6.0 miles. The top gives the rider a panoramic view of Santa Fe, the Rio Grande Valley and Lake Peak 1.0 miles to the north. Return to your car by the same route.

ASPEN VISTA

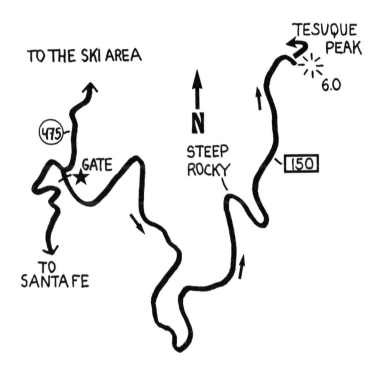

TO THE SKI AREA

475

GATE

TO
SANTA FE

N

STEEP
ROCKY

TESUQUE
PEAK

6.0

150

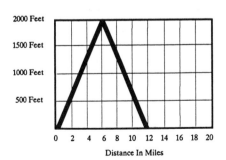

17   ELK MOUNTAIN

Total Distance:	*15.0 miles*
Riding Time:	*3-4 hours*
Elevation Gain:	*2000 feet in 7.5 miles*
Fitness Level:	*Advanced*
Riding Skill:	*Intermediate*
Maps:	*USGS 7.5' Elk Mountain, Santa Fe Nat'l Forest*

LOCATION & ACCESS:
Drive north on I-25 from the St. Francis exit in Santa Fe 16.6 miles and exit on the Glorieta/Pecos exit. Turn left and cross back over I-25 to intersect Highway 50. Turn right on Highway 50 and drive 6.0 miles to the town of Pecos. As 50 enters Pecos you come to a 4 way stop. Turn left here on Highway 63 and drive 12.6 miles to the town of Tererro (crossing the Pecos River on the bridge just before the store). After the store and bridge, Highway 63 turns into a gravel road. Drive .8 miles on the gravel and turn right on dirt road 646. (CAUTION: Don't pass this usually unmarked road. A half mile further up 63 is road 645 which goes up Elk Mountain but is not passable for most cars). Drive up road 646 for 3.5 miles and where it forks, go left downhill. At 5.3 miles there is a 3 way fork, take the left fork heading downhill. Park 1 mile past this junction. This road continues for another 1/2 mile but is generally unpassable due to several car swallowing mud holes.

ROUTE DESCRIPTION:
As you ride up 646 the road quickly is blocked and turns into a two track through the aspens and then a single track. At 1.0 miles from the start, the single track intersects Forest Road 156. Turn right and begin up the very steep and rocky road. At 2.8 miles from the start, at a saddle, you reach a 3 way junction. Take the left hand fork that goes along the ridge. At 5.8 miles from the start, turn right down the Elk Mountain road. This road begins as a rocky descent but soon begins to climb. At 6.6 miles from the start, a fork goes off on the right, keep left or straight. The top (11,661) is reached at 7.5 miles from the start. Views from the top of the Truchas Peaks, Santa Fe Baldy, Pecos Baldy, Hermit Peak and dozens of other mountains are excellent. Return to the car via the same route.

ELK MOUNTAIN

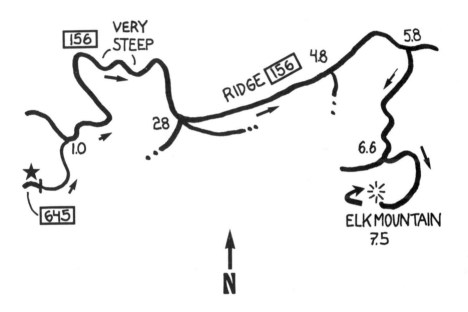

156 | VERY STEEP

RIDGE 156 | 4.8

5.8

28

1.0

645

6.6

ELK MOUNTAIN
7.5

N

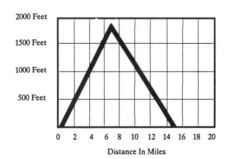

2000 Feet

1500 Feet

1000 Feet

500 Feet

0 2 4 6 8 10 12 14 16 18 20

Distance In Miles

18 LAMY RAILROAD SINGLE TRACK

Total Distance:	*25.0 miles*
Riding Time:	*4 hours*
Elevation Gain:	*200 feet in 12.0 miles*
Fitness Level:	*Beginner*
Riding Skill:	*Beginner*
Maps:	*USGS 7.5' Seton Village, Galisteo, Santa Fe, Santa Fe Nat'l Forest*

LOCATION & ACCESS:
Drive south on St. Francis Drive toward I-25, after driving 1/2 mile south of I-25 you intersect the frontage road. Turn right on the frontage road and drive 1/2 mile. After you cross the railroad tracks turn left onto a dirt road. Park immediately on the left behind some trees!

ROUTE DESCRIPTION:
Head south on the dirt path on the left side of the tracks. This path stays near the tracks most of the way, but almost always is far enough away that you aren't riding on the gravel rail bed. At 1.0 miles from the start the path crosses over the tracks to the right hand side of the rails. Now there are many short fast arroyo crossings for the next several miles, as the trail winds through the trees on the mesa (still near the tracks). This section of the ride is one of our favorite single tracks. The banked turns make going fast the only option. At 6.7 miles from the start you cross back over the tracks to the left side again, and ride near the houses of the Eldorado sub-division. At 7.3 miles from the start you cross the paved residential Aveninda Vista Grande. This is an optional turn around point. The riding further on is good but not as fun as the first section. Continuing on you cross dirt roads at 10.2 and 10.8 miles. At 12.6 from the start you intersect Highway 285. Lamy is just ahead. Turn around here and return to the car via the same route.

LAMY RAILROAD
SINGLE TRACK

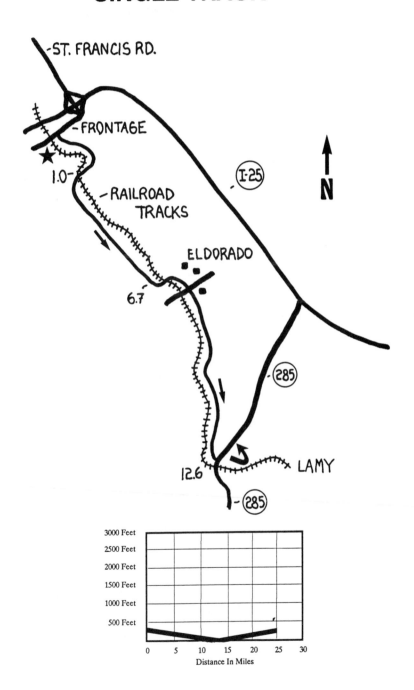

19 GUAJE CANYON

Total Distance:	*13.7 miles*
Riding Time:	*3 hours*
Elevation Gain:	*1750 feet in 6.7 miles*
Fitness Level:	*Intermediate/Advanced*
Riding Skill:	*Intermediate*
Maps:	*USGS 7.5' Guaje Mtn, Puye, Santa Fe Nat'l Forest*

LOCATION & ACCESS:
Start by locating Los Alamos High School on Diamond Drive in Los Alamos. Drive north on Diamond Drive approximately 2.2 miles and turn left on Guaje Pines Cemetery Road, opposite the golf course. Park at the upper end of the cemetery on the dirt road where the pavement ends.

ROUTE DESCRIPTION:
The ride begins at the cemetery where the pavement turns to dirt. Here there are two dirt roads. Take the road on the right that parallels the back side of the cemetery. This road starts off downhill but becomes very steep in .1 of a mile. At .7 miles from the start you will reach the top of the first steep climb. The road levels out and there is a road on the left, proceed straight ahead. The second steep climb comes shortly after. You reach the top of this climb at 1.3 miles from the start. Here another small road crosses the road you are on. Proceed straight ahead riding downhill. At 2.0 miles from the start you pass the Guaje Ridge Trail #285 on your left. Proceed downhill straight ahead and hold on. The descent becomes much steeper and the final descent into Guaje Canyon is **very** steep and rocky. You reach the bottom of Guaje Canyon at 3.3 miles. When you reach the intersection at the bottom of the canyon turn right onto Forest Road 442 and ride along the stream for 4.0 miles. At 7.4 miles from the start you will reach the junction of roads 442/416. Stay right on Forest Road 442 which continues down Guaje Canyon. After riding .7 miles look for Forest Road 57 on your right by a big pumping station. The junction of roads 442/57 is 8.1 miles. Turn right and begin to ride up Rendija Canyon. At 10.6 miles you will pass a small road on the right which loops back into road 57 in another .5 miles. Beyond a shooting range, at 11.6 miles the gravel becomes pavement. The road climbs a steep hill and intersects Barranca Rd at 12.4 miles. Turn right at this intersection (now residental). Make another right onto Diamond Dr. at the next stop sign. Ride down Diamond Dr. and turn right onto Guaje Pines Road and back to your car.

GUAJE CANYON

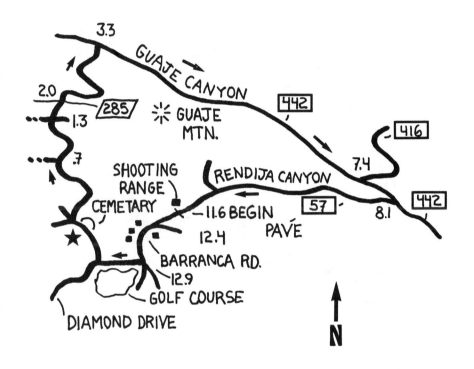

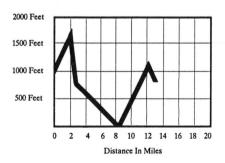

RIO CHAMA

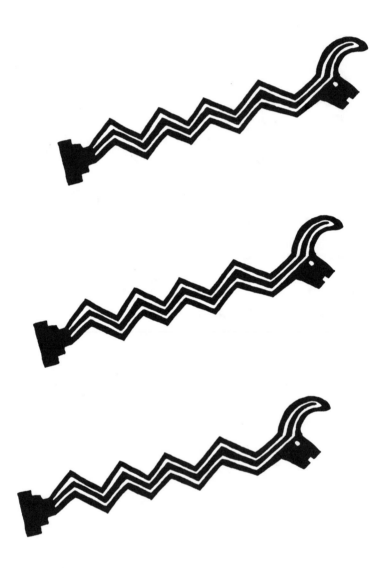

RIO CHAMA

This section of north central New Mexico is little traveled and much misunderstood. Geologically, ethnically, and culturally it is a remote and independent region of proud individuals. The small towns in this area are inhabited by families who can trace ownership grants back to the King of Spain. People in these towns aren't always excited to see outsiders. In north central New Mexico we always try to stay out of trouble.

The ride up the Rio Chama Canyon is one of our favorite canyon country rides. The red sandstone cliffs contrast sharply against the deep blue sky. Riding around Cabezon Peak gives one ample opportunity to reflect on man's relative insignificance. This peak is sacred to the Navajos and many pueblo tribes. When you are riding around White Mesa be sure to get off your bike, and hike and explore in some of the BLM wilderness study areas. This is a premiere winter riding area. When you ride to the end of Golondrina Mesa and walk out to the edge of the cliff you enter the dangerous realm of still quietude where it is very difficult to return unmoved. This is the point where the red waters of the Rio Chama and Rio Gallina merge with your soul. At the edge of the San Juan basin, Gallina Peak rises in defiance of its geologic legacy. This is a great ride for the geology enthusiast. For beautiful, remote country, ride along the edge of the sagebrush valley of the Rincon Colorado. This is a ride for people who want to be alone.

This part of New Mexico seems to be lost in time, when you look around from one of many high points you seem to be in some sort of primeval land. And that is exactly what keeps attracting us back for more and more. The incredible beauty of the land, complete with lost valleys, big views, indian ruins, hot springs, big plates of enchiladas and great mountain riding - is all a mountain biker could ask for.

RIO CHAMA OVERVIEW MAP

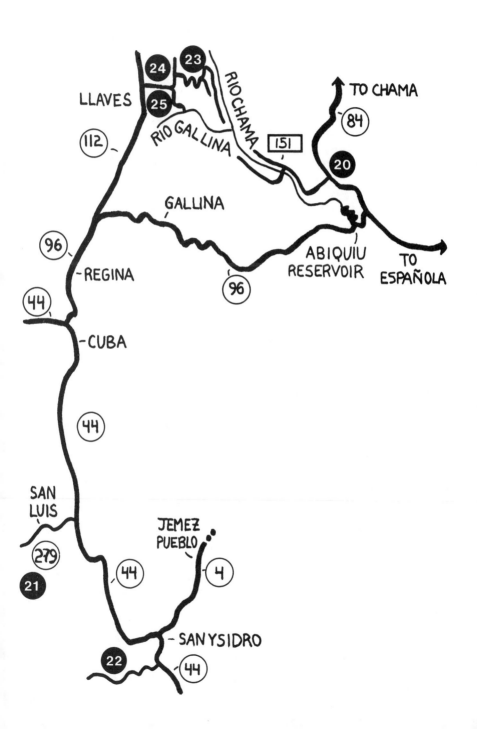

20 RIO CHAMA CANYON

Total Distance: 27.4 miles
Riding Time: 3-4 hours
Elevation Gain: 200 feet in 13.7 miles
Fitness Level: Intermediate
Riding Skill: Beginner
Maps: USGS 7.5' Laguna Peak, Echo Amphitheater,
                    Santa Fe Nat'l Forest
Notes: See Special Notes Section

LOCATION & ACCESS:
Drive north from Santa Fe on Highway 285 23 miles to Espanola. Turn left in Espanola on Highway 84 towards Chama. Drive north on 84 past the small town of Abiquiu. At 37.4 miles from Espanola, one mile past the Ghost Ranch Living Museum, turn left on Forest Road 151. Park at this junction.

ROUTE DESCRIPTION:
Ride up the smooth gravel road 151 as it heads across the mesa towards the Rio Chama. Be sure to enjoy the views of Pedernal Peak on the left. Within a few miles the road drops down next to the Rio Chama and the canyon walls are closer and higher around you. At 7.9 miles from the start you come to the only bridge across this section of the Rio Chama. Turn left here and cross the bridge. On the far side of the bridge the road forks, go right. Now this road heads up the Chama Valley parallel to the river and parallel to the road on the other side. Keep riding up the river along the rolling dirt road as it passes through the beautiful river bosque. At 13.7 miles from the start the road enters private land. Turn around here and return to your car on the same route you entered.

RIO CHAMA
CANYON

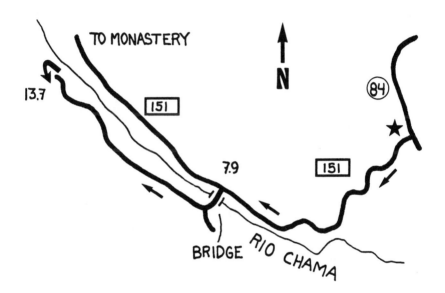

TO MONASTERY

N

13.7

151

84

★

7.9

151

BRIDGE

RIO CHAMA

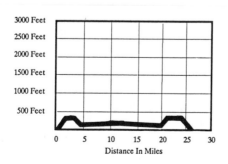

3000 Feet
2500 Feet
2000 Feet
1500 Feet
1000 Feet
500 Feet

0   5   10   15   20   25   30
Distance In Miles

21 CABEZON PEAK

Total Distance: *22.2 miles*
Riding Time: *3-4 hours*
Elevation Gain: *500 feet in 5.0 miles*
Fitness Level: *Advanced*
Riding Skill: *Beginner*
Maps: *USGS 7.5' Cabezon, San Luis, Guadalupe*

LOCATION & ACCESS:
Drive north on I-25 and exit on Highway 44 west out of Bernalillo towards
Cuba. At 41.8 miles turn left on the dirt road 279 heading towards San Luis
and Cabezon. Drive in past the old village of San Luis (notice the Penitente
morada on the right), and when the road splits at 13.0 miles from the
pavement, park.

ROUTE DESCRIPTION:
Start this ride heading down the left fork from the car. The road descends
towards the Rio Puerco, crosses the bridge, and then begins climbing
moderately. At 4.2 miles from the start turn left and keep climbing. Soon this
short climb is over and you are descending gradually. At 6.9 miles from the
car turn left again. This road climbs gradually up a valley and you come to a
fence and corral. Keep on straight passing a side road on the right side at 8.8
miles from the start. Come to another fence/gate at 10.7 miles from the start.
As the road climbs again at 12.0 miles from the start you pass a cattle guard
at the top of the climb and turn left. This is Ridge Road #1113. You pass a
cattle guard at 12.7 miles from the start, then a fence/gate at 13.2. Be sure to
close all gates behind you so ranchers don't make trouble for other mountain
bikers. At 15.4 from the start you pass a side road on the left. Then you ride
on the narrow ridge that is the namesake of the road. Again at 17.2 miles pass
a side road on the left. At 17.3 miles from the start you pass a cattle guard
and then turn left onto the Pipeline Road. At 18.2 miles from the start pass
a side road on the right, and then another at 19.1. You have to recross the
Rio Puerco at 19.4 miles but this time there is no bridge, just a cement crossing
and some mud. At 19.8 miles you rejoin the main Cabezon road, turn left.
Proceed up the road passing a cattle guard and rejoining the car at 22.2 miles.

CABEZON PEAK

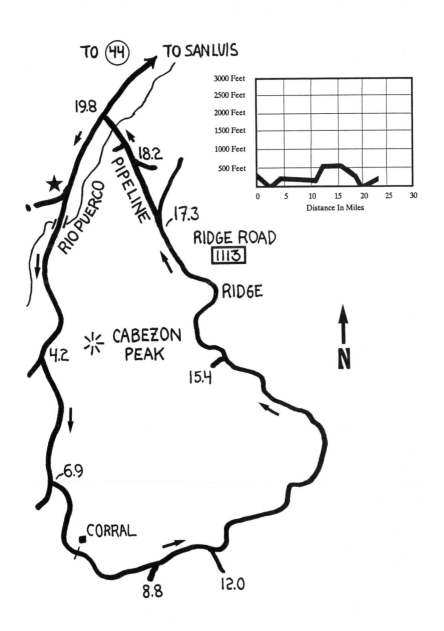

TO (44)   TO SAN LUIS

3000 Feet
2500 Feet
2000 Feet
1500 Feet
1000 Feet
500 Feet

0   5   10   15   20   25   30
Distance In Miles

19.8

18.2

PIPELINE

RIO PUERCO

17.3

RIDGE ROAD
1113

RIDGE

CABEZON
PEAK

15.4

N

4.2

6.9

CORRAL

8.8   12.0

WHITE MESA

Total Distance:	*16.0 miles*
Riding Time:	*2 hours*
Elevation Gain:	*200 feet in 6.0 miles*
Fitness Level:	*Beginner*
Riding Skill:	*Beginner*
Maps:	*USGS 7.5' San Ysidro, Sky Village NW*
	Sky Village NE

LOCATION & ACCESS:
Drive west on Highway 44 out of Bernalillo for 20.5 miles. Look for a gravel road to your left as you enter the big sweeping curve. This gravel road splits almost immediately. Take the left fork that has the Zia Reservation sign and drive on this gravel road for 4.0 miles until you reach a cattle guard and fence. This is the BLM boundary. The west side is public land. Park here.

ROUTE DESCRIPTION:
Begin this ride by riding west on the road you drove in on. This road winds its way through beautiful mesa country which is surrounded by the Ojito Wilderness study area. We recommend that you take a nice 8.0 mile ride down this main road, with frequent stops to hike and explore in the badlands formations that can be so inviting. This ride ends at 8.0 miles from the BLM boundry. The road continues on for several more miles and dead ends into a pipeline. We like to ride the 8.0 miles from the BLM boundary to a small rise that overlooks the Rio Puerco Valley. At this point you are able to see a nice view of El Cabezon from the south. There are many side roads to explore but remember some of these are closed to vehicular travel. Check with the BLM before you ride any side roads. Return via the same route.

WHITE MESA

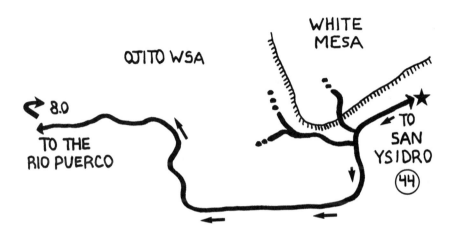

WHITE
MESA

OJITO WSA

8.0

TO THE
RIO PUERCO

TO
SAN
YSIDRO

(44)

N

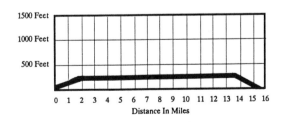

1500 Feet

1000 Feet

500 Feet

0 1 2 3 4 5 6 7 8 9 10 11 12 13 14 15 16

Distance In Miles

23 GOLONDRINA MESA

Total Distance:	14.4 miles
Riding Time:	3 hours
Elevation Gain:	800 feet in 7.0 miles
Fitness Level:	Intermediate
Riding Skill:	Beginner
Maps:	USGS 7.5' Llaves, Navajo Peak, Santa Fe Nat'l Forest
Notes:	Be sure to hike to the edge of the Golondrina Mesa to enjoy the view of the confluence of the Rio Gallina and the Rio Chama.

LOCATION & ACCESS:
Drive north from Cuba 3.4 miles on Highway 44. Turn right on Highway 96 and drive 12.8 miles. Turn left on Highway 112 heading towards El Vado Reservoir and drive 14.6 miles. Turn right on dirt Forest Road 7 and drive 1.3 miles. Turn right on Forest Road 6 (sometimes numbered 106) and drive 4.4 miles to a saddle and a 3 way intersection. Park here.

ROUTE DESCRIPTION:
At the 3 way intersection take the far left downhill fork. As you descend you pass road 107 on the left at .4 miles, keep straight. Pass road 505 on the left at 1.2 miles, again stay straight on 6/106. At 2.3 miles from the start the road forks, go left here. At 3.0 miles the road again forks, go right. At this point you switch from descending off of the flanks of Gallina Mountain to climbing up along Golondrina Mesa. From here there are some very rutted and rocky sections of road 6/106 but most are not steep. At 4.0 miles from the start the road splits, go right and at 4.3 it splits again. Go left here. If you become confused, remember you are on a pointed mesa and keep heading along it towards its tip. The end of the road is reached at about 7.0 miles from the start. Return via the same route you rode in on.

GOLONDRINA MESA

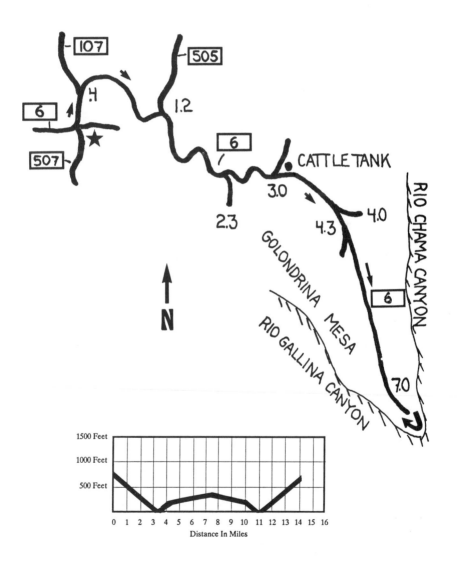

24 GALLINA PEAK

Total Distance:	15.0 miles (19.0 miles with side trip to the peak)
Riding Time:	*3-4 hours*
Elevation Gain:	*1800 feet in 5.0 miles*
Fitness Level:	*Advanced*
Riding Skill:	*Intermediate*
Maps:	*USGS 7.5' Llaves, Santa Fe National Forest*
Notes:	*See Special Notes Section*

LOCATION & ACCESS:
Drive north from Cuba 3.4 miles on Highway 44. Turn right on Highway 96 and drive 12.8 miles. Turn left on Highway 112 heading towards El Vado Reservoir, and drive 14.6 miles. Turn right on dirt Forest Road 7 and drive 1.3 miles. This is the intersection of roads 7 and 6, with 6 on the right. Park here.

ROUTE DESCRIPTION:
Ride up road 6 (which has signs saying 106 along it) climbing up the flanks of Gallina Mountain. After 4.4 miles of steep climbing a saddle is reached. At the saddle is a 3 way intersection. Take the far left fork which is still 6 (106) and descend .4 miles. At 4.8 miles from the start turn left on road 107 and begin to climb again. This road climbs for awhile and then begins to descend at about 6.5 miles from the start. At 6.8 miles from the start road 508 branches off on the right. This is the road to the summit of Gallina Peak (8929 ft). It is 2 miles to the summit with some steep climbing but mostly it is moderate. We recommend this side trip for the spectacular view of the Rio Chama, Perdernal Peak and Canjilon Mountain. After the side trip (or if you skip it) resume descent down 107 for another 5.2 miles of fun downhill and switchbacks. Intersect road 7, 12.0 miles from the start, at the bottom (this distance does not include side trip) road 7 has the same number dichotomy as road 6 (road 7 or road 107). Go left on 7 and ride the flat 3.0 miles back to the car.

GALLINA PEAK

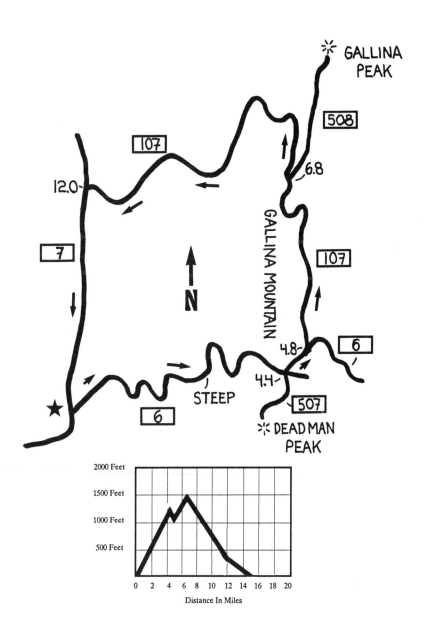

25 RINCON COLORADO

Total Distance:	*14.0 miles*
Riding Time:	*3 hours*
Elevation Gain:	*1100 feet in 7.0 miles*
Fitness Level:	*Intermediate*
Riding Skill:	*Intermediate*
Maps:	*USGS 7.5' French Mesa, Llaves, Santa Fe National Forest*
Notes:	*See Special Notes Section*

LOCATION & ACCESS:
Drive north from Cuba 3.4 miles on Highway 44. Turn right on Highway 96 and drive 12.8 miles. Turn left on Highway 112 heading towards El Vado Reservoir, and drive 14.6 miles. Turn right on dirt Forest Road 7 and drive .9 miles. As road begins to bend to the left, turn right on dirt two track and park.

ROUTE DESCRIPTION:
Proceed south (straight ahead) on the two track you parked on, passing some gates and corrals. At 2.7 miles the road enters the Rio Gallina Canyon and splits. Go right downhill to the river. The road now crosses the river several times in the next few tenths. At 3.1 miles from the start take the steep rocky right hand uphill turn. This is road 1293, which climbs at times steeply but mostly moderately, up the edge of the Gallina River Canyon. All along this section of the ride there are indian ruins and spectacular views. The last mile of this climb is the steepest and the rockiest. The top is reached 6.3 miles from the start where 1293 intersects Forest Road 8. Go right here down road 8 for only .4 miles and look for road 1292 on the right. If you go right down a very steep hill into the Rincon valley you missed the 1292 turn. 1292 stays on top for only a short distance then begins a full descent that lasts 3 miles. Rejoin 1293 at 10.7 miles from the start. Turn left here backtracking down 1293 to the Rio Gallina, turn left and ride back out to car as you came in.

RINCON COLORADO

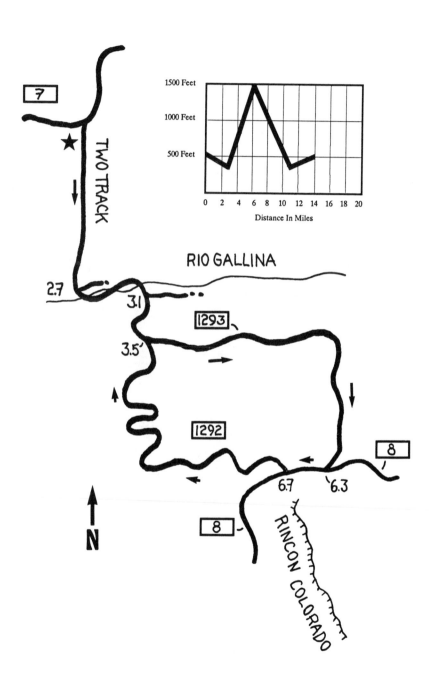

1500 Feet
1000 Feet
500 Feet

0 2 4 6 8 10 12 14 16 18 20
Distance In Miles

7

TWO TRACK

RIO GALLINA

2.7

3.1

1293

3.5′

1292

8

6.7   6.3

8

N

RINCON COLORADO

TAOS

TAOS

The rides in the beautiful Sangre De Cristo Mountains are among the best we have ever ridden. The views of the snow capped peaks and the abundant wildlife, including deer, elk, grouse, wild turkey and bears will renew your spirit and make this a special pilgrimage.

Most of the rides in this area are only accessible from June to October due to the deep snowpack in these high mountains. The Garcia Park ride takes you into the heart of this region but is relatively easy to ride. There is a beautiful aspen meadow inGarcia Park. Look for the numerous beaver ponds along the Rio Chiquito. The ride up Maestas Ridge is very long and is quite steep in some sections. The single track portion of the Quintana Pass ride is smooth and fast with lots of sharp turns. This single-track is definitely worth the hard work to get there. Amole Canyon is an area that was developed for cross country skiers but it is also a good place for beginning riders to learn the skills and gain the fitness needed to finish some of the harder rides. For fans of high mountain single track riding through beautiful flower filled meadows the Policarpio single track epitomizes the very best of mountain biking.

The great riding is only one of the reasons to visit the Taos area. Taos has long been a haven for artists and writers and there are many galleries and shops in which to spend some of your hard earned cash. Taos Pueblo is a beautiful traditional southwestern pueblo. If you have questions or need to rent a bike go see Joe Quintana at Native Sons Adventures.

TAOS OVERVIEW MAP

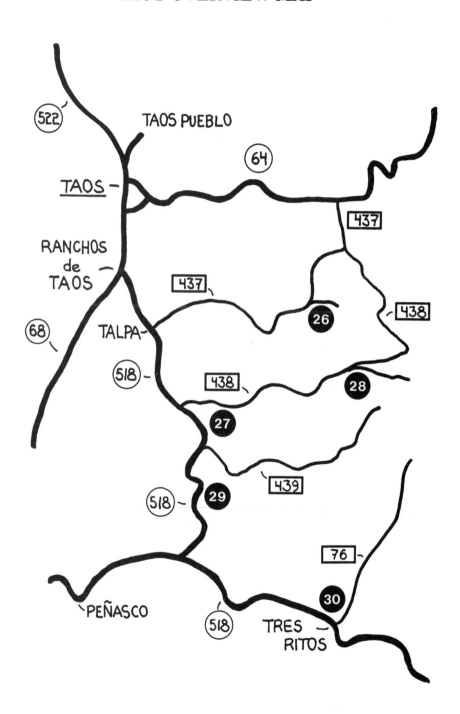

26 GARCIA PARK

Total Distance:	*14.0 miles*
Riding Time:	*3 hours*
Elevation Gain:	*1500 feet in 5.0 miles*
Fitness Level:	*Intermediate*
Riding Skill:	*Intermediate*
Maps:	*USGS 7.5' Shady Brook, Osha Mountain, Carson Nat'l Forest*

LOCATION & ACCESS:
Drive south out of Ranchos De Taos on Highway 518 for 2.0 miles and turn left on Forest Road 437. Drive up 437 for 11.0 miles along the Rio Chiquito. Park at the intersection of Forest Road 437 and 478, 11.0 miles from the pavement.

ROUTE DESCRIPTION:
From your car ride up road 437 for .4 miles. Turn left here climbing uphill. This is still road 437 heading uphill steeply towards Garcia Park. At 2.9 miles from the car you enter a large meadow (The Park). Here the road divides. Take the right fork, road 438 heading towards Borrego Crossing. Road 438 descends for several miles until you reach the Borrego Crossing of the Rio Chiquito at 7.1 miles from the start. Cross the stream and continue up 438 for 2.5 miles until you reach the Puertocito at 9.7 miles from the start. There is a 3 way junction here, go right; the sign says "Osha Park 441". You descend 441 and at .7 miles, 441 splits off on the left. Stay right on Forest Road 478. Descend down the steep rocky switchbacks of 478 for another 3.0 miles. At the bottom you re-cross the Rio Chiquito and reach your car at 14.0 miles.

GARCIA PARK

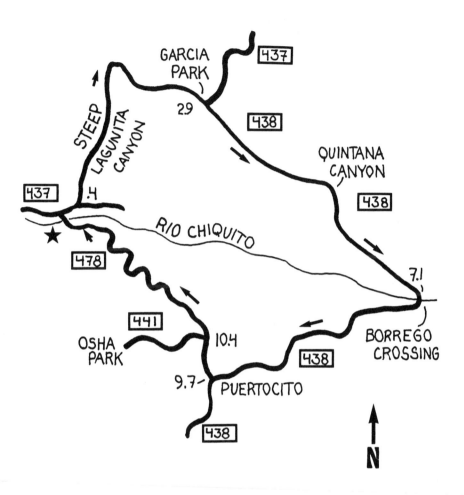

GARCIA PARK

437

438

29

STEEP

LAGUNITA CANYON

QUINTANA CANYON

438

437

.4

RIO CHIQUITO

478

7.1

441

10.4

OSHA PARK

BORREGO CROSSING

9.7

438

PUERTOCITO

438

N

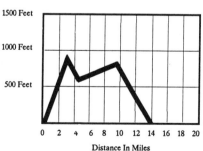

1500 Feet

1000 Feet

500 Feet

0 2 4 6 8 10 12 14 16 18 20

Distance In Miles

27 MAESTAS RIDGE

Total Distance: 26.0 miles
Riding Time: 5-6 hours
Elevation Gain: 3,100 feet in 7.0 miles
Fitness Level: Advanced
Riding Skill: Intermediate
Maps: USGS 7.5' Ranchos De Taos, Tres Ritos, Cerro Vista, Shady Brook, Carson Nat'l Forest

LOCATION & ACCESS:
Drive south out of Ranchos De Taos on Highway 518 for 7.0 miles and turn left on dirt Forest Road 438. Only drive about 50 yards on 438 and then turn right on Forest Road 440. Park here at this junction.

ROUTE DESCRIPTION:
This ride begins heading up very steep road 440 as it makes its way up Maestas Ridge. Along the ridge there are many side roads, but the main 440 is usually obvious. Pass roads on the left at 2.2, 4.5, 5.2 and 6.6 miles, stay right. The top of the first section of climbing is reached at 7.1 miles and offers excellent views of Wheeler Peak. Now there is a section of mixed ups and downs. Pass a road on the right at 9.1, stay left on downhill. At 9.6 miles from the start pass a road on the left, stay right. Forest Road 439A.1 splits off on the right at 10.0, stay left on Forest Road 440. After another 1/2 mile (10.5 miles from the start) is an important intersection - go right here up the very steep 439A. The top of Maestas Ridge is reached at 11.5 from the start. Keep going on 439A over the top, down the other side on the very steep and rocky switchbacks. Pass side roads on the left at 12.1 and 12.2 miles, stay right down the steep 439A. At 13.2 miles from the start, at the bottom of the descent you intersect road 439. Turn right here and descend 439 along the banks of the beautiful Rio Grande Del Rancho. At 14.2 pass the road to U.S. Hill on the left, but stay right going down along the Rio. Now enjoy the long descent on 439, passing a bridge at 22.8 miles from the start. Highway 518 is reached at 24.7 miles from the start. Turn right and descend 1.3 miles on pavement back to 438. Turn right here and go 50 yards then turn right to the car.

MAESTAS RIDGE

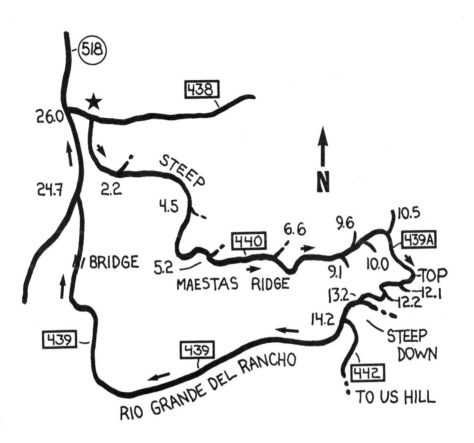

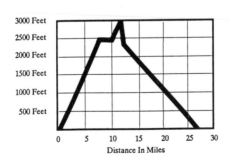

3000 Feet
2500 Feet
2000 Feet
1500 Feet
1000 Feet
500 Feet

0   5   10   15   20   25   30
Distance In Miles

28 QUINTANA PASS SINGLE TRACK

Total Distance:	*17.0 miles*
Riding Time:	*4 hours*
Elevation Gain:	*2000 feet in 7.0 miles*
Fitness Level:	*Advanced*
Riding Skill:	*Intermediate*
Maps:	*USGS 7.5' Osha Mountain, Shady Brook, Carson Nat'l Forest*
Notes:	*See Special Notes Section*

LOCATION & ACCESS:
Drive south out of Ranchos De Taos on Highway 518 for 6.9 miles and turn left on Forest Road 438. At .3 miles the road splits, stay right on 438. Now as 438 climbs along the Rito De La Olla several roads split off on the right. At 2.7, 6.3, and 8.2 miles along 438, stay left. At 10.0 miles park at the junction of 438/153.

ROUTE DESCRIPTION:
Begin ride heading up road 153 (the right fork where you parked) paralleling the Rito De La Olla. Along this section of road 153 there are many intersections where smaller side roads split off. To navigate this section refer to the map above for the many intersections. Road 153 climbs steeply for 4.0 miles at which point it intersects road 153B. Go left uphill over the saddle, most of the steep climbing in this ride is over. At 6.3 miles from the start begins a descent around to the north - watch closely here. At 7.2 miles the road 153 turns to the right heading down off of Osha Mtn. Go left here on a two track that climbs up off of the turn. This two track has some steep rocky climbs. At 8.1 miles from the start you pass over the ridge and begin to descend towards Trail #164. Pass a gate and fence line at 8.5 miles, again watch closely. At 8.8 (.3 past fence) the road turns to the left, go right, straight into the meadow full of down fall timber. As you look down across this meadow there is no road or trail. You must carry your bike down across this meadow and find the Quintana Pass Trail #164 at the bottom. Now you descend down several miles of the best single track around. You will reach Quintana Pass at 10.6 miles from the start, go left on road 438 mostly descending towards the Rio Chiquito. At 12.8 miles from the start, cross the Rio Chiquito at the Borrego crossing. Now 438 climbs gradually up to the Puertocito at 15.2 miles. This is a 3-way intersection. Turn left and ride 1.8 miles back to your car.

QUINTANA PASS
SINGLE TRACK

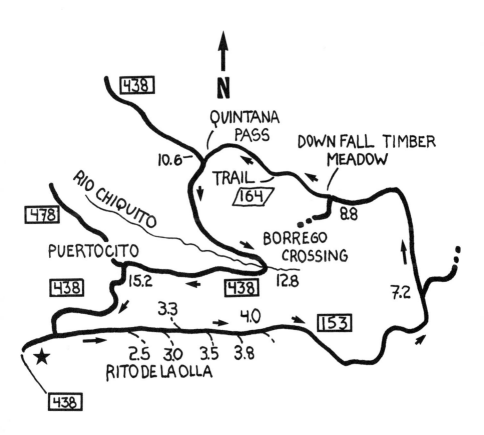

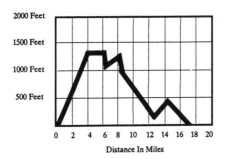

Distance In Miles

29   AMOLE CANYON

Total Distance:	4.0 miles
Riding Time:	1 hour
Elevation Gain:	800 feet in 2.0 miles
Fitness Level:	Beginner
Riding Skill:	Beginner
Maps:	USGS 7.5' Tres Ritos, Carson Nat'l Forest

LOCATION & ACCESS:
Drive south out of Ranchos De Taos on Highway 518 for 14.3 miles. Park on your left by the entrance to the Amole Canyon Nordic Ski Area.

ROUTE DESCRIPTION:
This area has recently been developed for cross country skiing and offers the beginner mountain biker the opportunity to gain the skills and endurance to attempt more difficult rides. The Amole Canyon ski area is a series of short linked loops. Although we have chosen just one, there are several other rides that are just as enjoyable. Don't hesitate to ride and explore for as long as you want. To start the Amole Canyon loop, ride up the main road approximately 1.0 miles where the road forks. Go right and ride for another .2 miles where you will reach a gate. Pass the gate you will skirt a big meadow and climb a short but very steep hill. The top is 1.5 miles from the start. At the top go right. The left fork drops steeply and dead ends. Proceed on the right fork and ride on old logging roads. The road becomes faint in this section but continues with some occasional berms across it as it gradually descends back to the main road. Just 50 yards before this road intersects the main road it becomes very faint. Continue downhill through the trees. At 3.0 miles intersect the main road. Turn left and ride 1.0 miles downhill to the car.

AMOLE CANYON

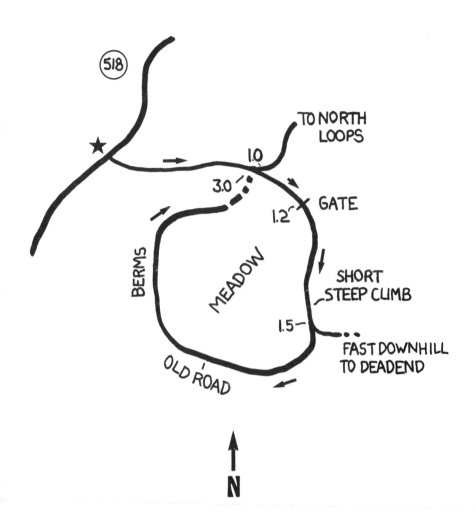

518

TO NORTH
LOOPS

1.0

3.0

GATE

1.2

BERMS

MEADOW

SHORT
STEEP CLIMB

1.5

OLD ROAD

FAST DOWNHILL
TO DEADEND

N

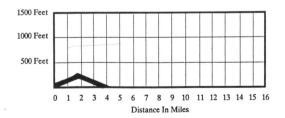

| | | | | | | | | | | | | | | | | |
1500 Feet
1000 Feet
500 Feet

0 1 2 3 4 5 6 7 8 9 10 11 12 13 14 15 16
Distance In Miles

30

POLICARPIO
SINGLE TRACK

Total Distance: *14.5 miles*
Riding Time: *3-4 hours*
Elevation Gain: *1300 feet in 6.0 miles*
Fitness Level: *Advanced*
Riding Skill: *Advanced single track/Intermediate road*
Maps: *USGS 7.5' Cerro Vista, Tres Ritos, Carson Nat'l Forest*

LOCATION & ACCESS:

Drive south out of Ranchos De Taos on Highway 518 for 8 miles, going over U.S Hill. At the intersection of Highway 518 and Highway 75 go left toward Tres Ritos staying on 518. When you reach Tres Ritos turn left on Forest Road 76 (La Junta Canyon Rd). Park at the pavement/dirt junction.

ROUTE DESCRIPTION:

Ride along road 76, 2.0 miles up the gentle hill. Turn right at the Duran Canyon Campground and cross the Rio La Presa on the bridge. Ride up road 76A along Duran Creek. The road climbs up the steep, rocky roadbed and at 4.1 miles from the start (2.1 on 76A) the road ends. Go straight ahead on the old road through a fence and into the large meadow. The road is very hard to follow here but goes up the right side of the meadow. At 5.1 miles from the start you pass an old log cabin in the meadow. Keep going uphill along the meadow and soon the road becomes more clear. Another mile past the cabin up the meadow (6.1 miles from the start) you intersect Forest road 722. Turn left on this wide logging road and ride only .4 miles and turn left on an old two track heading down a meadow at 6.5 miles from the start. This two track disappears in the large meadow that you enter. Cross the meadow to the far side and intersect Trail #13 at 7.5 miles from the start. Turn right and ride up Trail #13 along the treeline. Trail #13 soon enters the forest again and at 8.0 miles from the start you cross an unnumbered road. Cross the road and continue on the single track and enter another meadow at 8.3 miles from the start. Look for Trail #13 heading down a very steep hill on the left towards Policarpio Canyon. At the bottom of the hill the trail crosses a road. Stay on #13, down along the stream. Now you begin 2 miles of some of the best single tracking around. The trails crosses the stream several times and at 10.5 miles you intersect a road. Go right and cross the Rito De La Presa on the bridge and intersect road 76. Turn left and ride 4.0 smooth miles to the car.

POLICARPIO
SINGLE TRACK

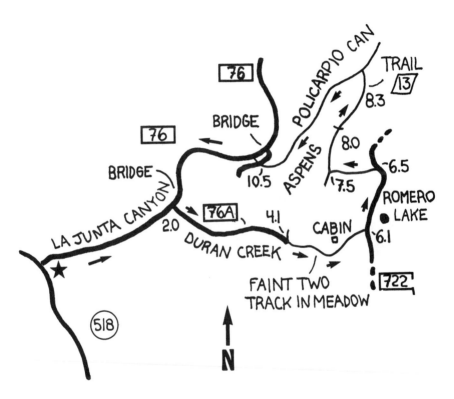

76

POLICARPIO CAN

TRAIL 13

8.3

76 BRIDGE

8.0

BRIDGE

10.5

ASPENS

6.5

7.5

ROMERO LAKE

76A 4.1 CABIN 6.1

2.0

LA JUNTA CANYON

DURAN CREEK

FAINT TWO TRACK IN MEADOW

722

518

N

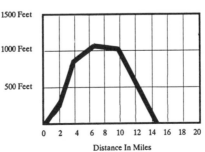

1500 Feet

1000 Feet

500 Feet

0 2 4 6 8 10 12 14 16 18 20

Distance In Miles

RED RIVER

RED RIVER

For a long time many New Mexicans have been avoiding Red River because of its reputation as a tourist hang out. We suffered from this idea also, but when we began researching this area we found one of the most beautiful and friendly areas in northern New Mexico. Red River is surrounded by mountain streams, alpine lakes and the highest mountains in the state.

Our favorite ride in the Red River area is the Goose Lake ride. This is a very difficult ride, climbing steeply for 3,000 feet up to Goose Lake at over 11,700. But the hard effort is worth it as soon as you begin down Goose Creek single-track. For an easier, but still advanced ride, try Middle Fork Lake. The climb up to this lake is very steep but it is only half as long as the Goose Lake climb, and Middle Fork Lake is exceptionally beautiful. The Old Red River Pass ride is much easier and offers the best views of the Taos range and Wheeler Peak. We went out looking for the Midnight Meadows ride, drawn in by the mysterious name, and again found a wonderful ride. This ride also has some high altitude climbs up steep rocky mountains, but the verdant aspen meadows and distant views of unknown peaks numb the ache in your legs and delivers transcendence.

As the crow flies, the Valle Vidal is very close to Red River, but by car it is a pretty good drive. On the way, you pass through some beautiful remote villages lost in the hidden valleys of northern New Mexico. The Valle Vidal is one of the crown jewels of our state and was the private playground of an elite rich few until 1982. The Costilla Pass ride takes the rider up through the Valle Vidal itself and is a good intermediate ride into a splendid backcountry area.

RED RIVER OVERVIEW MAP

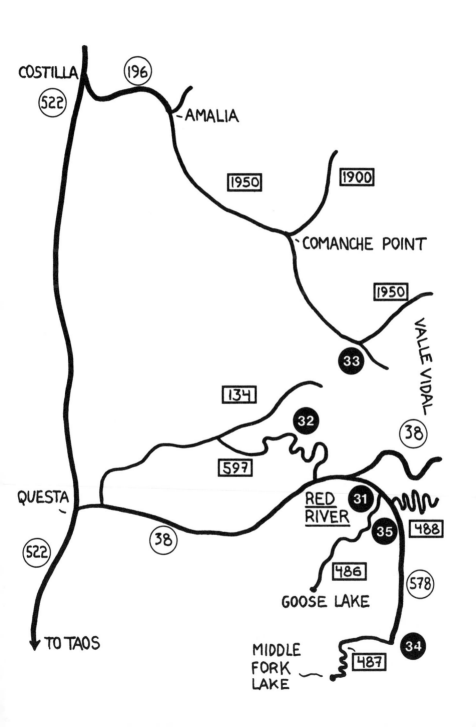

31 GOOSE LAKE SINGLE TRACK

Total Distance:	*15.3 miles*
Riding Time:	*3-4 hours*
Elevation Gain:	*3,000 feet in 8.0 miles*
Fitness Level:	*Advanced*
Riding Skill:	*Intermediate/Advanced on single track*
Maps:	*USGS 7.5' Red River, Carson Nat'l Forest*
Notes:	*See Special Notes Section*

LOCATION & ACCESS:
From the east end of Red River drive 3/4 of a mile on road 578. Turn right on Forest Road 486 and park just off of pavement in wide area on your left.

ROUTE DESCRIPTION:
Ride up 486 from the car and cross the Red River on the bridge. At this point 486 begins climbing very steeply up a very rocky road bed. Along 486 there are several side forks, but the main road is obvious. At 5.0 miles from the start the road forks, take the left fork that remains as 486, from here the climbing isn't as steep and the lake is reached at 8.0 miles. Now you can return down the road that you came in on, or go down the Goose Creek Trail #65. This trail leaves from near the outhouse at the lake, then after a few tenths, the trail splits, go left down along the creek. At times the trail is very hard to follow but always is near the creek. At 11.2 miles from the start (3.2 from the lake) the trail splits, take the right fork that goes towards the creek (the other climbs up ridge away from creek). The bottom is reached at 13.5 miles, cross bridge on the left and go left down 578 and 1.8 miles to the car at road 486.

GOOSE LAKE
SINGLE TRACK

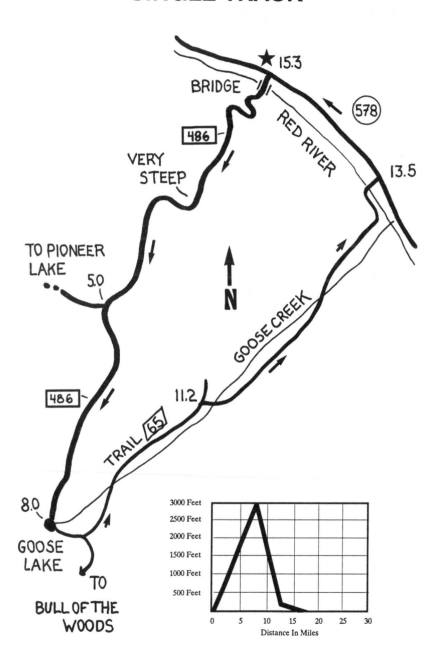

32 MIDNIGHT MEADOWS

Total Distance:	*18.8 miles*
Riding Time:	*4 hours*
Elevation Gain:	*2500 feet in 7.0 miles*
Fitness Level:	*Advanced*
Riding Skill:	*Intermediate*
Maps:	*USGS 7.5' Red River, Red River Pass, Latir Peak, Comanche Point, Carson Nat'l Forest*
Notes:	*See Special Notes Section*

LOCATION & ACCESS:
Turn off of Main St. in Red River on Mallette Road heading northeast. This is basically opposite the ski area. This is Forest Road 597, drive up it 5.3 miles to a saddle that has a Greenie Peak/Midnight Meadows sign on the right. Park here.

ROUTE DESCRIPTION:
The Midnight Meadows Trail leaves on the right where you parked on 597 and forks after 10 yards. Go right downhill. This road descends steeply for 1.3 miles, where you turn left uphill on the Greenie Peak Road. This road now climbs steeply and you pass a side road on the right at 1.5 miles from the start. At 2.2. miles is another fork, go right. At 2.4 miles yet another, go left. At 3.1 miles another, go right. At 3.5 miles from the start (after a short, very steep section) a fork is reached, go left up another very steep hill. This steep section ends the hard climbing until the very end of the ride. The road is now numbered 54 and at 4.5 miles from the start you reach a junction in a small meadow. Go left uphill towards the top of Greenie Peak. The peak is reached at 5.4 miles from the start at 11,249 feet. On top is a 3 way junction, go right which remains as 54 and descends from the top. At 6.3 miles from the start intersect 54C and go left downhill towards the Midnight Meadows. Descend through beautiful meadows and reach the junction with the Cabresto Road #134 at 8.1 miles. Go left down along Cabresto Creek on the broad gravel road. At 14.3 miles turn left on road 597 heading up Bonita Canyon towards Red River. The car is reached after 4.5 miles of uphill, for a total of 18.8 miles.

MIDNIGHT MEADOWS

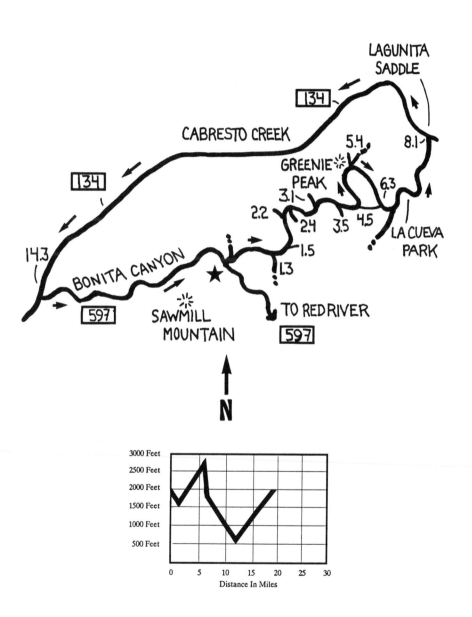

33 COSTILLA PASS

Total Distance:	*13.0 miles*
Riding Time:	*3 hours*
Elevation Gain:	*700 feet in 7.5 miles*
Fitness Level:	*Intermediate*
Riding Skill:	*Beginner*
Maps:	*USGS 7.5' Red River Pass, Comanche Point, Carson Nat'l Forest*
Notes:	*See Special Notes Section*

LOCATION & ACCESS:
Drive west out of Red River on paved road 38, 12.8 miles to the town of Questa. Turn right (heading north) on road 522. Go 20 miles to the small town of Costilla and turn right on paved road 196. Proceed up road 196 11 miles, at which point it becomes gravel. Proceed another 8 miles and turn right on the Valle Vidal/Shuree Lakes Road #1950. Head up 1950 4.5 miles and turn right down a small dirt road with a dirt parking area .4 off the main road. Park here.

ROUTE DESCRIPTION:
Ride out of parking area past locked gate on the two track road along Comanche Creek. At 1.8 miles the road forks, go left through the gate and past Clayton Camp. If gate is locked you need only go around and rejoin road on the left past the ranch house. After the ranch the road becomes faint and covered by grass. After you pass a narrows; 2.8 miles from the start watch for a faint road heading up on the right. This is 1.0 miles past the ranch house. This road climbs up the edge of the Valle Vidal towards Costilla Pass. At 3.5 miles from the start this road intersects another old road. Turn left here. Now the road parallels the edge of the Valle Vidal and offers execellent views of one of New Mexico's most beautiful places. Costilla Pass is reached 7.5 miles from the start. Now descend off the back of Costilla pass and pass a locked gate on the left, and a side fork on the left at 8.4 miles from the start. After this the road climbs back towards the north. At 8.8 miles from the start you reach a 3 way fork. Take the low road on the right that goes down the Comanche Creek drainage. On the way down you pass several side roads, but the main road is obvious. At 11.5 miles from the start you arrive back at the Clayton Camp. Go left here and return along the two track to your car.

COSTILLA PASS

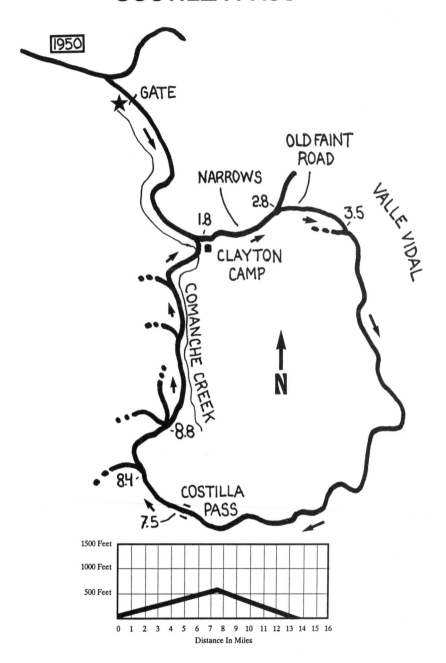

34   MIDDLE FORK LAKE

Total Distance:	*6.0 miles*
Riding Time:	*2 hours*
Elevation Gain:	*1500 feet in 3.0 miles*
Fitness Level:	*Advanced*
Riding Skill:	*Intermediate*
Maps:	*USGA 7.5' Wheeler Peak, Carson Nat'l Forest*

LOCATION & ACCESS:
Drive east out of Red River on road 578 for 6.5 miles to the end of the pavement and park.

ROUTE DESCRIPTION:
From the end of the pavement take the dirt road on the right (487) and begin gentle uphill along the Middle Fork. After about 1 mile up this road turn left and cross the Middle Fork on a bridge. This is still 487 but is labeled Trail 91 (Trail 91 actually forks away from 487 in 1 mile). After the bridge the climbing becomes very steep up many switchbacks. At 2.0 miles from the start Trail 91 splits off on the left, stay right on road 487 and cross the stream. Now you are on the last mile to the lake, which is the steepest. The lake is reached at 3.0 miles from the start and sits in a beautiful alpine bowl at 10,845 feet. There are many excellent hikes from the lake into the Wheeler Peak wilderness. Return to the start by the same route.

MIDDLE FORK
LAKE

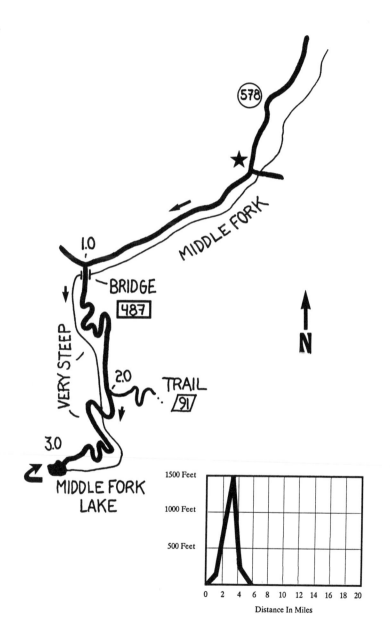

35   OLD RED RIVER PASS

Total Distance:	*12.2 miles*
Riding Time:	*2-3 hours*
Elevation Gain:	*1200 feet in 4.0 miles*
Fitness Level:	*Beginner/Intermediate*
Riding Skill:	*Beginner*
Maps:	*USGS 7.5' Red River, Red River Pass*
	Carson Nat'l Forest

LOCATION & ACCESS:
This ride starts from the east end of Red River at the junction of Highways 38 and 578.

ROUTE DESCRIPTION:
Ride up paved road 578 1.2 miles and watch for the old Red River Pass road on the left. Turn left here (488 is Old Pass road) and begin the climb up the pass. This road goes up a series of switchbacks which are not steep but are continuous. The top (9854 ft) is reached 4.3 miles from the start (3.1 on dirt). At the top turn right on road 490, heading towards 4th of July Canyon. Road 490 has several short but very steep uphill sections, however the rest of 490 is moderate or downhill, with many excellent views of Wheeler Peak and the Taos range. At 6.7 miles from the start (5.5 on dirt) turn right and head down 4th of July Canyon. This is a short but very fast descent. Paved road 578 is intersected at 7.7 miles, go right returning to the start, for a total distance of 12.2 miles.

OLD RED
RIVER PASS

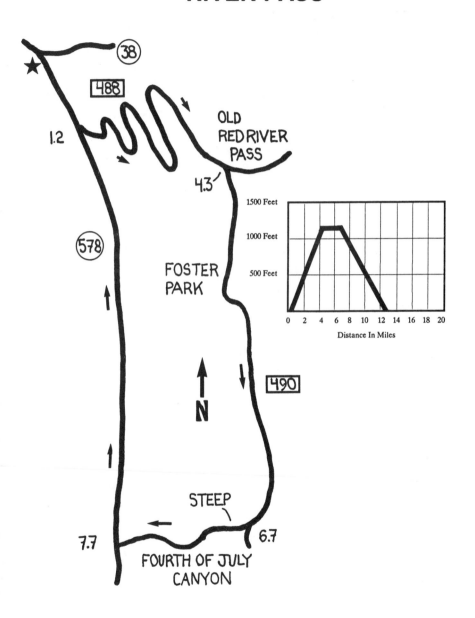

SPECIAL NOTES

RIDE # 14 GLORIETA BALDY SINGLE TRACK
The USGS 7.5' McClure Reservoir map does not accurately represent Trail #272. You should consult the Santa Fe Nat'l Forest map or use the map in the text for trail information. At the 16.9 mile point you will encounter a gate marking the Baptist Convention Center boundary. It is legal to ride through the Center as long as you close the gate and stay on the main road.

RIDE # 13 GLORIETA MESA
There are a myriad of great two-track roads branching off from Forest Road 326. They all make good rides, but because they all look similar riding them may present navigational difficulty.

RIDE # 29 AMOLE CANYON
This small area was initially developed for cross country skiing and therefore has many short loops. We chose only one to be included in this book. There are many others that are also good to ride.

RIDE # 33 COSTILLA PASS
After you pass the ranch house and ride through a nar-rows, look for a faint road on the right (this is one mile from the ranch house). It is hard to find because it is a very faint grass covered road that climbs up and away on the right from the road you are on. To navigate this ride you must use the Carson National Forest map as it shows the entire route. The old USGS topographical maps are incorrect and do not even show the main access road #1950.

SPECIAL NOTES

RIDE # 31 GOOSE LAKE SINGLE TRACK
Trail # 65 down Goose Creek does not appear on the 7.5' Red River Map. It only appears on the Carson National Forest map. This trail is very faint and hard to follow at times, remember it parallels Goose Creek as it descends.

RIDE # 32 MIDNIGHT MEADOWS
Many sections of this ride do not appear on the listed USGS topographical maps. Use the Carson National Forest map for navigation. This map shows the entire route.

RIDE # 25 RINCON COLORADO
When we started compiling this book in 1989 the current Santa Fe National Forest map contained most of the roads in this ride. Now however, both the USGS maps and the updated Santa Fe National Forest map show very little of this ride. You must navigate by our directions and the map book.

RIDE # 24 GALLINA PEAK
There is a discrepancy on this ride between how the roads are numbered along the route and how they are numbered on the updated Santa Fe National Forest map. Road #6 on the updated map is numbered 106 along the route.

SPECIAL NOTES

RIDE # 11 EL CALDERON LOOP
The topographical maps for this ride show all of the roads except those between .8 and 2.4 miles. There are also some short sections of private property you must ride through. The authors inquired about the legalities of riding through these sections at the El Malpais Monument headquarters and this ride was suggested as one of the best in the area.

RIDE # 4 CEDRO PEAK SINGLE TRACK
Many of the single-track trails in this area do not appear on any published maps. The roads mentioned with Forest Service numbers are the only ones that do appear. This area is very confusing, you must pay attention to the mileage directions given in the ride descriptions.

RIDE # 3 LONE PINE SINGLE TRACK
Many of the single-track trails in this section do not appear on any published maps. The roads mentioned with Forest Service numbers are the only ones that do appear on the maps. This area can be very confusing so you must pay close attention to the mileage directions given in the ride descriptions.

RIDE # 20 RIO CHAMA CANYON
If you would like to ride in this area but the length of this ride seems too long, drive part of the way in on Forest Road 151. If you drive and park at the bridge crossing the Rio Chama it shortens the ride to 11 miles. Use caution in wet weather as the road is famous for truck stopping mud.

SPECIAL NOTES

RIDE # 28 QUINTANA PASS SINGLE TRACK
There are so many forks and side roads on parts of
this ride that we can't show them on the ride map or
describe them in the narrative. Watch closely for the
turn to the left off of road 153 at 7.2 miles from the
start. If you miss this turn it will send you miles down
road 153 in the wrong direction. The most difficult
navigation in this ride is at the 8.8 mile mark. Here
you enter a large meadow. Looking down across this
meadow there is no apparent trail or road, and is full
of down fall timber. You must carry your bike down
across the meadow where you will find Trail # 164 at
the edge of the clearing.

Ride Name	Fitness Level	Riding Skill	Road Surface
Alameda Bosque	Beginner	Beginner	Single-track
Glorieta Mesa	Beginner	Beginner	Dirt road
10K Loop	Beginner	Beginner	Dirt road
Amole Canyon	Beginner	Beginner	Dirt road
White Mesa	Beginner	Beginner	Gravel road
Lamy Railroad	Beginner	Beginner	Single-track
Mt. Sedgewick	Intermed	Beginner	Dirt road
Old Red River Pass	Intermed	Beginner	Dirt road
Golondrina Mesa	Intermed	Beginner	Dirt road
Garcia Park	Intermed	Beginner	Dirt road
Costilla Pass	Intermed	Beginner	Dirt two-track
Cerro Colorado	Intermed	Beginner	Dirt road
Rio Chama	Intermed	Beginner	Dirt road
Rincon Colorado	Intermed	Intermed	Two-track
Foothills Trail	Intermed	Intermed	Single-track
El Calderon Loop	Intermed	Intermed	Two-track
Cedro Peak Trail	Intermed	Intermed	Single-track
Quartz Hill	Intermed	Intermed	Two-track
Lone Pine	Intermed	Intermed	Single-track
Tablazon Canyon	Intermed	Advanced	Single-track
Cabezon Peak	Advanced	Beginner	Dirt road
Middle Fork Lake	Advanced	Intermed	Dirt road
Midnight Meadows	Advanced	Intermed	Dirt road
Gallina Peak	Advanced	Intermed	Dirt road
Quintana Pass Trail	Advanced	Intermed	Rd single-track
Guaje Canyon	Advanced	Intermed	Dirt road
Elk Mountain	Advanced	Intermed	Dirt road
Aspen Vista	Advanced	Intermed	Dirt road
Barillas Peak	Advanced	Intermed	Dirt road
Maestas Ridge	Advanced	Intermed	Dirt road
Glorieta Baldy	Advanced	Advanced	Rd single-track
Gooseberry Springs	Advanced	Advanced	Rd single-track
Goose Lake	Advanced	Advanced	Rd single-track
Faulty Trail	Advanced	Advanced	Single-track
Policarpio	Advanced	Advanced	Single-track

ENVIRONMENTAL REMARKS

Of the 10 million bicycles sold in the United States last year approximately 50% were fat tire mountain bikes. Mountain bikers are becoming an ever increasing presence in wilderness recreation areas. This increasing presence is causing dissention among traditional wilderness users. The key issues are the potential for mountain bikes to cause environmental damage, and the aesthetic impact of mountain bikes on public land and other areas where hikers or wildlife are present. There is a hiker biker conflict, and there are legitimate environmental concerns. You can help alleviate these problems by providing information about attractive alternative mountain bike routes like the ones in this book, and by following these simple rules:

1) Ride on designated trails only.
2) Stay off vegetation and muddy trails.
3) Yield right of way to slower trail users.
4) Ride in control and don't cut ruts.
5) Respect trail closures and "No Trespassing" signs.
6) Leave gates as you found them.
7) Practice "soft cycling" riding techniques.
8) Help teach new riders proper trail etiquette.

Remember future riders will be judged by our actions.

Best Rides

Garcia Park - Taos
Quartz Hill- Zuni Region
Costilla Pass - Red River
Rio Chama Canyon - Rio Chama
Glorieta Baldy - Santa Fe

Best Single-Tracks

Policarpio - Taos
Gooseberry Springs - Zuni Region
Quintana Pass - Taos
Lone Pine - Albuquerque
Goose Lake - Red River

Best Enchiladas

El Cafecito - Grants
Matildas - Espanola
Taoseno Cafe - Taos
Dave's Not Here - Santa Fe
Ron's Camino Real - Albuquerque

DISCLAIMER

All riders are cautioned to use prudence and good judgement in selecting proper equipment and the appropriate route on which they ride. Many factors may cause a given route to vary in its degree of difficulty from the time the authors rode it. Because the rider's equipment, age, bicycle experience and physical conditioning will greatly affect the rider's ability, the authors can assume no responsiblity for injuries resulting from any ride selected in this book.

RIO MOUNTAINSPORT
QUALITY OUTDOOR GEAR RENTALS

MOUNTAIN BIKE RENTALS

EXPERTLY MAINTAINED
HELMET INCLUDED WITH RENTAL

FULLY DECKED OUT FOR OFF-ROAD ADVENTURE
EACH BIKE EQUIPPED WITH:
DOUBLE WATER BOTTLE CAGES
FLAT RESISTANT TUBES
TOOL KIT
PUMP
GEL SADDLE

cyclometer

CONVENIENTLY LOCATED
ON RIO GRANDE BLVD
ONE BLOCK NORTH OF I-40

RIO GRANDE BLVD

X

I-40

MAPS & GUIDE BOOKS
CYCLING ACCESSORIES
IN-LINE SKATE RENTAL
LOCATED ONE MILE
FROM
OLD TOWN PLAZA
&
RIO GRANDE NATURE
CENTER

RIO MOUNTAINSPORT
1210 RIO GRANDE BLVD. NW
ALBUQUERQUE, NEW MEXICO 87104
505-766-9970

NOTES

NOTES